The End of Change

The End of Change

HOW YOUR COMPANY CAN SUSTAIN GROWTH AND INNOVATION WHILE AVOIDING CHANGE FATIGUE

PETER SCOTT-MORGAN
ERIK HOVING
HENK SMIT
ARNOUD VAN DER SLOT

McGraw-Hill

NEW YORK   SAN FRANCISCO   WASHINGTON, D.C.   AUCKLAND   BOGOTÁ
CARACAS   LISBON   LONDON   MADRID   MEXICO CITY   MILAN
MONTREAL   NEW DELHI   SAN JUAN   SINGAPORE
SYDNEY   TOKYO   TORONTO

Library of Congress Cataloging-in-Publication Data
 The end of change: how your company can sustain growth and innovation while
 avoiding change fatigue / Peter Scott-Morgan ... [et al.]
     p.   cm.
 Includes index.
 ISBN 0-07-135700-9 (cloth)
 1. Organizational change. I. Scott-Morgan, Peter.
HD58.8 .E53 2000
658.4'06—dc21   00-038685

McGraw-Hill
A Division of The McGraw-Hill Companies

                1 2 3 4 5 6 7 8 9 0   AGM/AGM   0 6 5 4 3 2 1 0

ISBN 0-07-135700-9

Printed and bound by Quebecor/Martinsburg

This publication is designed to provide accurate and authoritative information in
regard to the subject matter covered. It is sold with the understanding that neither the
author nor the publisher is engaged in rendering legal, accounting, or other professional service. If legal advice or other expert assistance is required, the services of a
competent professional person should be sought.
—*From a Declaration of Principles jointed adopted by a Committee of the American Bar
Association and a Committee of Publishers*

McGraw-Hill books are available at special quantity discounts to use as premiums and
sales promotions, or for use in corporate training programs. For more information,
please write to the Director of Special Sales, Professional Publishing, McGraw-Hill, Two
Penn Plaza, New York, NY 10121-2298. Or contact your local bookstore.

This book is printed on recycled, acid-free paper containing a minimum of
50% recycled de-inked fiber.

Contents

PART 3   TEAMS, QUALITY, AND COMMUNICATION

PART 4   THE BIGGER PICTURE

Preface

The danger of using the word "NO" to a consultant is that it provokes the consultant to respond one better . . .
Of course, it all started innocently enough:

Peter: People may like change, but no one likes to *be* changed. Managers have been ramming change down people's throats and now companies are starting to suffer from change fatigue. It doesn't need to be that way. Between us we've all seen ways to help companies avoid that.

Erik: Mmmmm, No. It's not as simple as that. Companies have no choice. Things like the Internet are forcing the pace of change. Consultants are brought in to speed up change, not slow it down. Maybe we should combine our experiences of how to manage change more efficiently.

Henk: No! People need stability. Not everything needs to speed up. We need to agree which parts of the company need to change and which bits we should leave alone. These days, if people get sick of being changed they may leave the company. We have to focus on how companies can keep their people by providing relative stability despite the turbulence of the outside business environment.

Arnoud: NO! The ultimate reason stability is important is the financial benefits it brings—it avoids the inefficiencies that occur when people suffer change fatigue. But the business performance is why you have to do it. It's not just a "luxury" to keep your people. We should combine experiences on the ways companies can maximize performance by creating a sort of dynamic stability.

Henk: No, that's right. Think about it. Consultants are always being placed in different projects, on different locations, working with a different team and with different clients, and still they can remain extremely motivated. It's a sort of dynamic stability. There's not really any change fatigue.

Peter: No—because it's business as usual. It's even exciting. That's why it feels stable. It doesn't feel like real "change."

Erik: No, but when consultants are told to move desks or change procedures or there's a reorganization, *then* there's enormous resistance. *That* still feels like real change. So it's nothing to do with consultants, only that in the consulting profession some things have been built into business—as usual so they don't cause the change fatigue they would in other organizations.

Arnoud: No, exactly, and that's just one of the ways companies can avoid the perception of constant change. R&D labs do it totally differently. We should catalog all the different approaches. See the pattern. Write the approaches up in a manual. No, an article. No, better, a book. What do you think? I think it's a great idea!

Henk, Erik, Peter: NNNNOOOOO!!!

Three months later we banned the use of the word "NO" in any of our further discussions. But by then the damage was done, and we'd all been sucked in . . .

To be fair, having become committed to the idea, actually writing the book took quite a while. Not just because we could work on it only on weekends and in our spare time. But because there is no more skeptical audience than a group of consultants, so almost every suggestion whether it related to a proposed business model or the time to take a break for dinner resulted in a major debate. And those discussions were *such* fun. So much so that we are now rather disappointed to realize that we've all but finished the book.

We write this Preface at the transition to a new millennium. It's the holiday season. And as we see people bringing initially rather drab fir trees into their homes, putting them up, trimming and decorating them, and generally transforming them, we think of all the people who helped improve *The End of Change:*

- The support for the tree came from the Rotterdam office of ADL which kindly picked up our bills. Thank you Jacques.
- Trimming and major decoration was performed by Josh Mills, who cut the branches to size and covered up the worst flaws.
- The decorations themselves were provided by various colleagues who contributed insights and examples for several of the chapters (Jochem; Taco; Thijs; Sebastiaan; Femke; Nienke).
- The lights and candles came from Frits Lauterbach, who enlightened us by being our friend and coach.
- And the shining star at the top of the tree was the gift of Martijn van der Mandele, who helped us through troubling times by assuring that we never lost our vision and inspiration. (And thanks for saving the title!)

Then, of course, there are those special people standing around the tree that loved the whole exercise so much that they made us promise that we would never do anything like it again. The same group that encouraged us to start the book even though they knew they would only get to spend more time with us once the book was finished. Without their support we'd never have kept going. Without their hints that "enough is enough" we might never have finished. It is to these loved ones that the tree is dedicated:

Francis
Elianne and Fleur
Mireille
Carolien.

Introduction

Escaping the Change Dilemma

A vicious spiral is swirling through the corporate landscape. Inexorable worldwide pressure for performance is leading to accelerating change initiatives, which result in greater disruption, which makes it more difficult to change, which builds the pressure for performance, which leads to more initiatives. . . .

As a result, corporate leaders find themselves on the horns of a dilemma. Their companies need to change faster and faster, yet their employees' energy for change is becoming exhausted. As employees suffer from change fatigue and yearn for less disruption, executives are driving for ever-greater change.

Companies worldwide have to compete on their ability to change faster and more effectively than their rivals. Whether the innovation is in strategy, processes, products, services, or organization; whether the innovation is implicit or an advertised differentiator; whether the company knows it or not, aggressive and accelerating innovation has become the leitmotif of the twenty-first century. The Fortune 500 companies are currently spending twice their profits on change. Yet they're satisfied with only half the results.

It won't get any better any time soon.

Current levels of change initiatives are almost certain to increase dramatically. The drivers for change, such as the convergence of information, computing, and communication, will continue to grow and feed off each other. Geopolitical borders will continue to evaporate, stimulating a truly global economy. The effects of these drivers are amplified by the emergence of the new e-business economy. In 2002, the Fortune 500 companies plan to spend almost $1 trillion on change initiatives. These, they expect, will disrupt almost all of their employees.

In principle, all this activity might be fine, as well as inexorable. In practice, the growing disruption caused by change is simply not sustainable. Disruption drains financial resources. Disruption drains people. Organizations have to be wrenched out of a stable situation, moved, then pushed back into stability. Each oscillation in and out of stability disrupts the organization, leading to cumulative change fatigue. That undermines the ability of the company to compete. Many top executives, midlevel managers, and shop-floor workers tell us they're already tired of change. They are finding it progressively more difficult to sustain innovation, let alone accelerate it.

Companies now estimate that 70 percent of their employees will be disrupted by change initiatives in the next 3 years. Many companies say that bringing about a given change is increasingly difficult. Compounding these pressures, no best practices have been established for coping with, let alone thriving in, never-ending turbulence. How can organizations escape this approaching disaster? How can they thrive in the increasing turbulence of the global economy? How can they avoid accelerating into unsustainable disruption—yet still keep innovating ahead of their competitors? How can they ensure sustainable high performance in the unpredictable environment of the world economy? How can they remain flexible and responsive without suffering from change fatigue and burn-out?

After 7 years of grappling with these questions, our answer is: Innovative companies should not fixate on change; they should concentrate on maximizing stability, with the innovation built in. To thrive within turbulence, an organization has to maximize what we call "stable innovation." This takes different forms in different circumstances.

Let's look at how we arrived at this conclusion.

When you consider all the pressures on businesses today and how best to categorize them, we find that the most practical differentiators of the innovation required are frequency of innovation and level of innovation.

Frequency of innovation (the horizontal axis), stretches from relatively low frequency—maybe every 2 or 3 years—to high frequency, potentially every few weeks or even every few days. The level of innovation (the vertical axis) stretches from a low level—where you know how to do the change and there's nothing fundamentally innovative required—to the extreme of totally uncharted territory. There, you need to address a sort of change you've never seen before, and everything about it requires deep innovation.

Each of these four broadly defined categories of the business environment has a fundamentally different pattern of innovation:

- Incremental innovation, appropriate for environments that are only occasionally disrupted, and then by factors that the organization knows how to deal with.

- Spasmodic innovation, needed when organizations only occasionally have to deal with one-time change, and there's a big

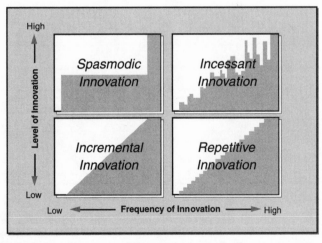

Figure I.1 Innovation map. There are broadly four categories of business environment that demand fundamentally different patterns of innovation.

pulse that goes through the organization as it shifts from one form to another.

- Repetitive innovation, best for organizations that face frequent change of a recurring nature, one after another after another.

- Incessant innovation, for organizations that face fast and furious changes they've never experienced before, with challenges coming from all directions.

Each of the four categories needs its own practical structure to optimize performance by minimizing disruption. We call these stability structures:

- Pyramids maintain stability in an environment of incremental innovation, following a strategy of slow adaptation and occasional avoidance.

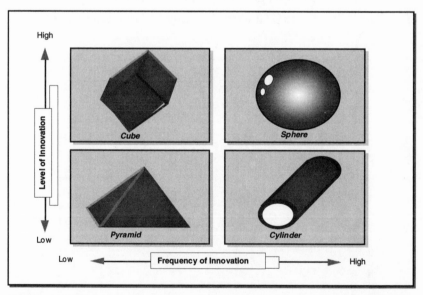

Figure I.2 Stability structures. For each pattern of innovation there is a practical structure that optimizes performance by minimizing disruption.

- Cubes maximize periods of stability by clustering spasmodic innovation into short, efficient bursts.
- Cylinders minimize disruption by building repetitive innovation into their processes.
- Spheres reduce disruption amid incessant innovation by developing the maximum number of options, then selecting the most stable.

To get a feel for these structures, imagine that each is about a meter tall and made of solid concrete. You're trying to move them along the ground.

A Pyramid is the most difficult structure to move. It sits solidly on its broad base and is difficult to rock. The only way to move it is by nudging it along, but there's a lot of resistance. It's hard, perhaps impossible, to move it very far very fast.

The Cube is also stable, firmly on its base. To move it you push in just the right place and get it to pivot on its edge. Keep applying the pressure and it will roll over into a new position. To move it more, you need to apply pressure once again, pivot it up, and keep pushing until it rolls over.

The Cylinder, on the other hand, is easy to move, so long as it's rolling on its long axis. Try pushing the cylinder in any other direction and it's nearly as difficult as shoving at a Pyramid or Cube. Once the Cylinder is rolling, you can gently steer it—but only gradually.

The Sphere, of course, is relatively easy to move in any direction and can be steered as it is rolled. Change the direction as often as you like. Compared with the other structures, it's highly mobile. Yet, like the other structures, the Sphere cannot be moved up and down—so it's not fully mobile.

These four stability structures map onto exactly the same axes as the innovation map: frequency of innovation and level of innovation. Where there's low frequency of innovation and low level of innovation, the optimal structure is a Pyramid. An example might be the

World Bank or a British Petroleum oil refinery. Where the frequency of innovation is low but the level of innovation is high, the appropriate structure is a Cube, like the National Aeronautics and Space Administration (NASA) during the Apollo space program or perhaps today's British Army. Where frequency of innovation is higher but the level of innovation remains low, the best stability structure is a Cylinder. Consider the core operations of Calvin Klein or Intel, geared for 6- and 18-month cycles, respectively. Where frequency of innovation and level of innovation are both high, the appropriate structure is a Sphere. Sony's research and development (R&D) department or a hospital emergency room are good examples of a Sphere.

But always remember: although it's tempting to categorize an entire organization as one structure or another—the World Bank as a Pyramid, for example—that's not the whole picture. While an organization may have one dominant structure, most have a portfolio of different structures (finance departments in almost any company, for example, are nearly always Pyramids). And indeed, that's precisely our point. Each company needs a portfolio of structures. With this portfolio in place, an organization can sustain high performance and foster innovation with a minimum of disruption. Remember that disruption is ultimately felt by people, so to minimize their feelings of disruption, management must address what is driving their perception in the first place.

In our view, this portfolio of structures and the advantages it confers is central to maximizing stability in a time of change, and thereby avoiding accelerating into the dilemma. We'll examine these structures in more detail in the coming chapters.

Part 1

Stability Structures

CHAPTER 1

The pyramid

**Encouraging incremental innovation
for those who can prepare in advance**

The key words to remember about Pyramids are *perfection* and *continuity*. A best-practice Pyramid is not, as many people assume, the classic Pyramid that stands for everything static, hierarchical, and bureaucratic. Rather, the best-practice Pyramid remains stable, despite potential disruption in the environment, in four ways:

1. It encourages continuous incremental improvement.
2. It creates a buffer to absorb disruption, maintaining stability in the bulk of the organization.
3. It sometimes disables the disruptive influence.
4. On occasion, it constructs a more appropriate Pyramid next door to the existing organization.

Rather than being old-fashioned and rigid, the best-practice Pyramid smartly handles turbulence by preparing for it a long way ahead. Not every organization or part of an organization has the luxury of being able to prepare far in advance, but for those that can, the Pyramid structure is highly appropriate. It can be used where most turbulence is known and does not occur frequently. Another way of describing the Pyramid structure is *it doesn't rock the boat if it doesn't need to* (Figure 1.1).

The essence of the Pyramid is that plans tend to be very detailed, specific, and explicit. Career progression and the reward system are based on continuity in performing clearly described tasks. Risk taking is discouraged. The whole culture is strongly reinforced by formal, official, written rules that, like cement, bind the Pyramid together.

Of the four ways in which a Pyramid can remain stable amid potential disruption, the most natural is to encourage continuous incremental improvement. An excellent example of this is the Total

Strategy	• The strategy discussion focuses on the route to get to a goal that is deep seated in everybody, and therefore is taken for granted. • The leadership role is to constantly reinforce the strengths of the system and to recognize the contribution of details.
Process	• Plans are highly detailed and written. • Control is based on conformance to plan. • Financial management is designed for efficiency and cost saving.
Resources	• Personnel selection is based on proven track record (new role should almost already have been demonstrated). • Noncore competencies can be recruited into the company (little outsourcing). • Success is perceived in terms of sustained achievement; other main motivators for personnel are often status and belonging. • The reward system is based on continuity in performing the described tasks, and discourages risk taking.
Organization	• Empowerment is often constrained within the boundaries of a particular role. • Roles and functions are described clearly. • Training is organized around procedural descriptions of the roles and functions as well as "safe failing spaces" and simulators. • The values and unwritten rules are mutually strongly reinforcing and self-sustaining.

Figure 1.1 A best-practice Pyramid is not like the classic form that most people assume it to be.

Quality Movement (TQM) initiated in Japan by W. Edwards Deming and others in the early 1970s, for example, Toyota. Quality circles were set up in manufacturing companies, where teams created Ichikawa diagrams or fishbone diagrams and executed root-cause analysis to improve operations incrementally from the bottom up. This creates stability because the incremental improvements are not major disconnects and changes are smoothed into a gentle transition. Because techniques such as TQM are based on the input of those who will be affected by change, the participants are much less fearful of disruption than if change were imposed from the outside.

The second way that a Pyramid remains stable despite potential disruption is by creating a buffer that absorbs the disruption while maintaining stability in the main organization. Consider how IBM set up a "skunkworks" to develop the personal computer. In a fast-developing market for microcomputers, IBM was eager to follow Apple, Tandy, and Atari. Research and experience showed that collaboration with others and open standards were necessary to ensure success, but that was impossible within the IBM of the 1970s. Rather than banging their heads against a wall by trying to change the well-established mechanisms, the procurement system, and indeed the underlying culture, IBM's top management created a small group and grounded it outside the company's mechanisms. This miniorganization did not have to follow the same rules, policies, and procedures as the rest of the company. Hardware components were brought in from around the world. Microsoft was invited to develop the operating system and was able to dictate the appropriate hardware and budget with resources provided by IBM. Only when the product was fully developed and ready for production was the enterprise brought back into the operating framework of the company. Through use of this approach, IBM was able to successfully develop a product without disruption to its other operations.

The third way that Pyramids encourage stability is by disabling the disruptive influence. Microsoft provides an instructive example. The hugely successful company plays in a highly unstable and massively turbulent arena, with constantly changing playing fields, aggressive competitors, and new technologies coming to market almost daily. One way Microsoft deals with this is by organizing certain areas as Pyramids. For years, Microsoft remained atop the market by using its near monopoly on operating systems and its financial strength to ensure that certain parts of its company continued to grow and continued to be run as Pyramids, stable and without turbulence. One such Pyramid is Microsoft's system of distribution channels.

Microsoft did not (and does not) want its distribution channels worldwide to be structured in such a way that they had to address the new technologies, new products, and new countermeasures the company might need to deal with on other fronts to neutralize competitive threats. Microsoft created distribution channels—through retailers and computer makers who "bundle" in Microsoft software—so that whether Microsoft is selling Office 2000 or Word 97 or *Magic Schoolbus* children's software, the conduits remain the same, undisturbed by turmoil elsewhere.

The final way the Pyramid can maintain stability is by building a more appropriate Pyramid next door to the existing organization. General Motors' (GM's) strategy with the Saturn illustrates this approach. Faced with a flood of Japanese subcompacts that were conquering a niche in the U.S. market and cutting into its sales, General Motors concluded that it was simply too large and cumbersome to redefine itself to meet these challenges. Instead, GM set up a new company next door. Saturn was able to capitalize on the GM heritage and to draw on GM's resources without being restricted to the General Motors structure and its rules and conditions. Saturn also had its own labor force with its own contracts and agreements. This freedom allowed Saturn to be much more competitive with the Japanese companies: Saturn was able to focus on quality and customer satisfaction while being competitive on pricing, and it achieved a large initial success. By building this Pyramid next door, GM was able to shield the parent ship from disruption and still build a presence in a new and highly competitive market. The greatest disappointment of the Saturn innovation was that precious few of its innovations were transplanted or cross-fertilized into the parent company, as GM's strategic planners had anticipated. In many ways this justifies the original decision to set up Saturn separately—it would never have survived otherwise.

REFLECT.COM OF PROCTER & GAMBLE

Procter & Gamble (P&G) is one of the world's leading consumer goods companies with successful brands such as Pampers, Ariel, and Crest. During the 1980s and 1990s the company was one of the top performers on the stock exchange, making P&G a blue chip company. In the marketplace P&G's key strengths are seen as global

---

brand management, mass distribution, and production efficiency. Within the context of this book, P&G is in many of its processes a world-class Pyramid.

Durk Jager became head of P&G after 30 years with the company holding the senior management position in worldwide marketing, sales, and account management. Yet shortly after he accepted the CEO position, he came to the conclusion that the role he had trained for his whole career didn't exist any more.

He realized that the world was no longer about mass-market communication, but rather about personalized attention and care. He saw a world evolving where new start-ups have a global reach from day one, scale can be obtained without high investment, and price transparency in the market will rapidly lead to efficient global markets. Durk Jager realized that he could not begin to comprehend the impact of all these changes on Procter & Gamble. And he considered the old governance and management model of strong hierarchy and control incapable of directing, steering, and leading his large organization through the years to come. So what could he do?

As a Pyramid needs to do, he created a separate entity—called Reflect.com—built like a Sphere (explained further in Chapter 4) that would indirectly allow P&G to "play the numbers game" and experiment with using new media to access customers. P&G would stay in control by means of the venture capital funding of the initiatives. Durk decided that the only way to stay ahead in the new game P&G had to play was to experiment a lot, learn from all the experiments, and observe how the market evolved, while all the time remaining on top of it.

With Reflect.com, P&G is experimenting with personalized communication to its customers, marketing tailored products instead of one size fits all, and competing directly with its former key clients—the retail chains.

One thing that Durk has changed for himself is that formerly the coach-coachee relationship was from senior to junior employees. Today Durk asks for advice from the new young entrants into P&G.

Pyramids, by allowing only slow evolution, minimize feelings of disruption. Formal rules, policies, procedures, processes, and structures provide bulwarks. These are very well defined and clear and everyone knows them, so the formal structure gives people a feeling of slow or very little evolution. This is *not* a revolutionary environment. People tend to join Pyramids early in their careers and stay a long while, often until retirement. Given stable personnel, incremental improvement techniques such as in total quality prove very effective and internal systems are protected and buffered against external shocks. Substantial effort is maintained to reinforce the basic mental model of the Pyramid:

Professionalism = steady progression + no surprises

As you might expect, some people fit better into Pyramids than they do elsewhere. The ideal Pyramid individual enjoys sustaining and building strength and solidity. His philosophy is to "ride out any storm." Like most character traits, this one offers potential advantages and disadvantages, too. At best, the Pyramid individual is superbly reliable, capable of delivering whatever was promised on time and within budget. On the other hand, he or she can be stubborn, conservative, and narrow. (Later we'll consider the influence of other personalities on the structures they exist within, and whether and how they influence a company's migration from one set of structures to another.)

CHAPTER 2

The cube

An advanced way to deal
with occasional major change

C ubes maximize periods of stability by clustering changes into short, efficient bursts. The key words are *preparation* and *timing*. A best-practice Cube does not mimic the one-time disruptive change mechanism that has marked so many corporate environments in the last decade. Instead, the best-practice Cube is a far more advanced way of dealing with occasional major change (Figure 2.1). As with the Apollo missions to the Moon or today's British Army, there's a focus on overall objectives and a continual preparation for moving to the next stage. Potential feelings of disruption during the transition are minimized primarily by keeping the dominant structure of the organization constant.

Over the last decade most companies have been forced to go through one wrenching change after another. The typical sequence is to unfreeze the organization, push it through transition, then attempt to refreeze it. This process, first described decades ago by Kurt Lewin, has become known as a Lewin change. But in these times of never-ending turbulence, a Lewin change is increasingly irrelevant. No longer can a company complete the refreeze, then relax, consolidate, and enjoy a long period of calm. Relying on the Lewin model would quickly result in severe change fatigue.

The Cube, in contrast, never completely refreezes during calm. Because it does not, the next change is less wrenching. During the calm, the next transition is anticipated, perhaps identified and planned for. To maximize stability, the Cube tries to keep as many things constant as possible—before, during, and after the transition. (In a Lewin change, companies might find everything broken apart and changed into something different.)

Many details of a Cube indicate just how different it is from the wrenching change that most organizations have endured. Strategy

Strategy	• The strategy discussion focuses on the necessary one-off improvements. • The leadership needs to be able to shift modes, or leadership needs to be different during the period of consolidation and transition.
Process	• Planning is roughly determined by milestones and contingency plans during the transition and similar to the pyramid in the period of consolidation. • During transition, control is focused on the leaders, whereas during consolidation, broader feedback systems are used. • Financial management is geared to reserve for the unknown during and after the transition, as well as maximizing productivity during the consolidation period.
Resources	• Personnel selection is based on candidates' demonstrating the two sets of skills needed for periods of transition and consolidation. • The needed competencies for the transitions are mostly brought in (consultants), or shared between departments. • Success is perceived in terms of achieving a given transition as well as performance during the consolidation phase. • The reward system is based on contributions to the overall long-term objective.
Organization	• The level of empowerment toward the transition leaders is high. • The roles and functions are described in deliverables with vague boundaries of the interfaces between functions. • Training objectives are to maintain change readiness as well as efficiency during consolidation. • The values and unwritten rules encourage coherence to a common goal as well as resilience, efficiency, and professionalism.

Figure 2.1 A best-practice Cube does not use a classical Lewin change.

focuses on necessary one-time improvements, so planning becomes all important. Financial management is focused on creating a reserve to deal with the unknown and on maximizing productivity during periods of calm. People are chosen for their ability to manage not just during calm but also during transition—because both phases are part of business as usual. Training, therefore, has to maintain readiness for change as well as to enhance people's efficiency during the consolidation phase. The organization's values and culture have to encourage adherence to common goals, as well as resiliency and efficiency.

NASA during the 1960s was a classic Cube. It started major programs aimed, incrementally, at setting a man on the Moon. Mercury's goal was to orbit manned spacecraft, Gemini's to achieve prolonged space flight and docking in space, Apollo to enable lunar exploration, starting on the Moon's surface. During each program, the objective was reached through a sequence of projects that in the end rolled the Cube from one face to the next. Each project was aimed at taking the next step in the direction of the general objective, but the project itself was based on the situation at that moment. Significantly, the number of projects within a given program was not predetermined. The planners and managers were savvy enough to know that was simply not possible.

Over time, NASA's program grew ever larger, driven by a variety of factors—not least the "space race" with the former Union of the Soviet Socialist Republic (USSR). Public opinion, in part stage managed by NASA and the government that was funding it, came to see space exploration as a heroic activity. The huge arsenal of engineers and technologists who participated in NASA projects reached critical mass, spewing forth a technical drive that knew no boundaries and accepted no frontiers. This might have been extraordinarily disruptive, but stability was achieved by focusing on the overall objective and by building and reinforcing a team that was passionately focused on achieving that objective. Landing a man on the Moon and returning him safely to Earth was such an overarching objective, a commingling of technological virtuosity and unbridled imagination, that it inspired all those who worked on the program, as well as the spellbound public. Making the astronauts and the engineers part of a large core team that stayed throughout the programs provided considerable stability. Despite major setbacks, most notably the death of three astronauts in a prelaunch fire of the Apollo 1 mission in 1967, the team grew stronger and more committed to making its dream come true.

Another example of a Cube is the modern, professional British Army. During periods of calm, the army continually prepares for conflict, when it will have to rely on practiced models. Still built around the traditional regiments, the British Army is increasingly collaborating with the British Navy and the Air Force to create teams with complementary skills. In peace time—the calm—soldiers prepare for deployment in unknown environments and circumstances. They learn models and processes that are kept as simple as possible, and they rely on these. They learn to live by values and beliefs. Rather than learning "how to do something," they are continually trained to work independently within a framework of orders and drills as best practices, given an objective and a reason. They learn to trust the teams they operate in by creating a common vision and a definition of roles and responsibilities.

When deployed, soldiers find stability in relying on what they have been taught and perfected. Their models and processes provide stability and create the time for innovation. Everybody goes through the same logic very quickly, which makes any lengthy discussions unnecessary. A close connection is kept with reality—short communication lines with home, for example—to ensure that values are not forgotten.

Even under the toughest conditions, when lost in the bush or surrounded by a superior force, soldiers find stability by relying on their preparation. They are self-sufficient and comfortable with their personal equipment. They are physically prepared for the hardships and mentally trained to have the fullest confidence that they will make it through.

NOKIA: CONNECTING PEOPLE IN THE FORESTS

Today everyone thinks of Nokia as the leading brand in mobile telecommunications. But its heritage is very different. Long ago, in Finland, the roots of Nokia lie in forestry from which it diversified into tissue papers. Building on its strengths in forestry Nokia concluded that forestry equipment could also be an attractive business for it. So it moved full force into that business. The next business it entered was rubber boots and tires—no doubt because you need them in the forest.

The next logical step (at least in the minds of those steering Nokia) was to go fully into electronics equipment, specifically TV sets. However, perhaps having realized that you do not need those in a forest, Nokia subsequently divested its forest and forest equipment businesses.

Well, when you are the executive of a company in electronics equipment, wearing your company's rubber boots walking through the ubiquitous Finnish forest you just divested, you suddenly realize that what you really need is not a TV, but a mobile phone. If you need one, everyone who wears rubber boots needs one. So that is the next logical step.

This—or something like it—was the means by which Nokia became the no. 1 brand in mobile communications. In the early 1990s, when it became clear that GSM (global system for mobile) would become the European standard in mobile telephony, Nokia was prepared to jump onto it fully, both with infrastructure and handsets. Nokia was the first company to realize that a mobile phone would become one of the few things (next to keys and wallets) that people would carry around all the time. So it invested heavily in understanding what kind of services and design people on the move would want.

Nokia is now by far the largest and most successful supplier to the mobile customer. The question in our minds is: "What is the next business Nokia will surge into—after or before divesting their mobile business?" Could it become the largest Internet portal in the world?

Four hundred million users worldwide turning on their mobile telephones six times a day hitting the Nokia Internet homepage 2.4 billion times per day . . .

Nokia helps create stability for its people by inspiring the belief that whatever paradigm shift will follow, Nokia will be the first one to jump into it and be on top of it. It is the typical behavior of a Cube. Nokia has radically shifted its business focus over time. By performing these paradigm shifts, it has shown itself not to be afraid to radically divest from its previous core business. It has stayed, however, close to its core values of integrity, freedom in entrepreneurship, individuality, and teamwork. This fundamental bridging is key to providing continuity while going through paradigm shifts.

If we imagine what it's like to be within a Cube, we can see that potential disruption during transition is minimized primarily by keeping the dominant structure of the organization constant. An organization's structures and most of its important performance measures are largely maintained during, and on both sides of, the transition. So even as the Cube topples from one face to another, much of the power structure and the feedback mechanisms remain constant. What structures and performance measures are specific to the transition may have short-term priority, but longer term they are of secondary importance. In the Cube the mental model is

Professionalism = effective transition + efficient consolidation

The most valued character within the Cube is the one that enjoys regularly rebuilding the business and has the philosophy that "A laurel, rested on, wilts. . . ." At best, Cube individuals are courageous and decisive; at worst they can sometimes be almost brutal and disruptive. Their favorite saying is, "You can't make an omelet without breaking eggs."

CHAPTER 3

The cylinder

Maintaining continuity across cycles
to minimize disruption

Cylinders minimize disruption by building repetitive changes into their processes. The key words are *efficiency* and *learning*. Within a Cylinder, potential feelings of disruption are minimized primarily by maintaining continuity across the cycles.

The repetitive innovation processes needed in a Cylinder are built into an overall cycle that matches the *clock rate*—the dominant rate of repetition—of those disruptions. Although the Cylinder is very good at absorbing what otherwise would feel like disruption, it is not absorbing all disruptions—only those in the dimension for which the Cylinder was designed.

Not all repeating changes, however, are potentially disruptive to people, so not all cyclical processes are structured as Cylinders. The accounting cycle in a finance department, for example, is not a Cylinder, because starting another accounting cycle at the beginning of the year doesn't disrupt the people within the department: They are doing the same sorts of things with the same people, reporting along the same organizational structure. As we pointed out earlier, most finance departments are structured as Pyramids.

Because a Cylinder can be gently steered when it is moving, incremental innovations are possible, but they require a form of pattern recognition: You need to recognize the common denominators of those changes, whether they recur every 6 months or every year, so that they can be built into the Cylinder itself. These otherwise disruptive changes then become nothing more than business as usual.

In Cylinders, the strategy processes, resources, and organization are quite different from those of the Cube and the Pyramid. In the Cylinder, the focus is very much on the performance of the cycle and the ability to transform that cycle gradually (Figure 3.1). Leadership is focused on encouraging a sense of competition for improving best

Strategy	• The strategy discussion focuses on new applications of the cycle. • The leadership role is to create a sense of competition to improve the best cycle performance.
Process	• Planning is done for the duration of one cycle as well as across several cycles. • Control is based on lagging indicators of a cycle. • Financial management is geared to continuous improvement within the cycles.
Resources	• Personnel selection (typically for a whole cycle) is based on track record on previous cycles. • The needed competencies are available through content experts. • Success is viewed in terms of expertise, and the main motivator for personnel is normally being the best at what they do. • The reward system is based on performance in last cycle.
Organization	• The level of empowerment is high toward the leader of a cycle and low within the cycle. • The roles and functions are standardized. • Training is geared to standardize working methods so that switching between cycles becomes easy and improvements within cycles can be obtained. • The values and unwritten rules are geared to developing the best experts in necessary fields of expertise.

Figure 3.1 Best-practice Cylinders are not just cyclical processes.

cycle performance; financial management is geared to continuous improvement within the cycles. Success within a Cylinder tends to be viewed in terms of expertise, and training is geared toward standardizing work methods so that switching between cycles becomes easy and improvements within cycles are easier. All the values, culture, and written rules are geared toward developing the best experts in necessary fields of expertise.

One way in which the Cylinder manages to minimize disruption is by focusing on the steps and the responsibilities in the specific cycles. The semiconductor industry, where Moore's law was born, illustrates this nicely. Gordon Moore of Intel postulated that a chip's performance doubles every 18 months. Chip makers, then, must constantly renew their production lines. This puts pressure on the chip makers' suppliers to innovate ever faster. ASM Lithography (ASM-L), a Dutch company whose photolithography projection system, known as a *wafer stepper,* is used in the chip-making process, regularly comes up with newly designed machines through which its clients can continue to compete on the cutting edge of the "Moore cycle." Within ASM-L, management ensures that the design and development processes are focused on achieving the single most important objective: to come up with the newly designed machine. By focusing step by step on activities within the development cycle, everybody remains aware of individual responsibilities—and everybody is aware of the team goal.

How can ASM-L maintain stability while going through these cycles? It makes sure that employees are able to focus on their responsibilities within the different cycles by having detailed roadmaps for developing a line of products each 18 months. Developers are responsible for the different steps described in detail. Everybody knows what their challenges are. Product developers work closely together in a development team, and within that team changes are minimized.

The second way that Cylinders minimize disruption is by ensuring that within cycles people are using reasonably standard approaches and have responsibilities similar to those in other cycles and that people maintain a home base between cycles—tying into the same part of the organization from one cycle to the next.

An information technology (IT) implementation company applies these forms of stability. Many such companies are working with clients these days in implementing Enterprise Resource Planning (ERP) systems across a broad front. These implementation programs are huge in size, impact, scope, and cost. It often takes 6 months to 2 years to implement them. The work is performed at the client's site, and each project is very different in terms of scope, objectives, and specifics of business. Often, the project team's members vary from implementation to implementation. All this could be quite disruptive because the people involved in these projects are faced with new clients, a new task, a new environment, a new culture to work in, and a new location where they work for months at a time.

To provide stability to these employees, the companies involved apply standardized approaches and roles and provide a constant home base. All employees are trained to use the same methodology and the same structured approach in each project. The goal is for everyone to feel immediately comfortable as they start a new project. The roles and structures in the teams are standardized, so employees know exactly what is required from the start. By giving employees not only consistent coaching but the same director to evaluate them over each cycle, a sense that everything is standardized is created. By creating a home unit or home base, or a team at the IT company, the company provides stability despite all kinds of different objectives, roles, tasks, locations, clients, and cultures.

NASA in the 1990s minimized disruption in Cylinders by keeping teams and roles constant. Through a strong political and public lobby, NASA is able to ensure relatively stable budgets and has effectively disabled the spasmodic changes it had to suffer in the past. Rather

---

VODAFONE AND THE MOBILE POKER GAME

Since early 1999, when Vodafone acquired Airtouch and thus became the largest mobile operator in the world, mergers and acquisitions have significantly narrowed down the mobile playing field in Europe. Large players such as France Telecom, Deutsche Telecom, and British Telecom have been actively extending their footprint and building critical mass. SBC and Ameritech together have presence in no fewer than nine countries in Europe. Many small players have been taken over (Orange) or left the game (Cable & Wireless).

Staying behind is not a viable option for most operators, as acquiring critical mass will become necessary to maintain strong positions with suppliers and to rapidly deploy and replicate new services and products. It also enables international offerings with flat tariffs throughout Europe, which is increasingly demanded by the international traveling (business) community. In addition, economies of scale will enable cost savings in many areas, including product creation, purchasing, and operations.

To optimize cost savings, mobile operators are setting up their network operations as Pyramids and their new product creation as Cylinders.

In the current mobile operator world a consolidation game is going on with stakes that vary according to the acquisition candidates. This can be compared with playing on poker tables, where like in a casino the poker tables differ with respect to the maximum stakes. On the small table the stakes are limited; however, on the largest table (behind the curtain) the stakes are unlimited. You can only sit at the largest table if you have unlimited funds at your disposal (or you are able to bluff your way through it). Vodafone is still the only operator on the largest poker table with unlimited budgets, playing the mobile game on a global scale. Many of the supranational operators are on the medium poker table and have the potential to follow Vodafone, while the local players on the small table have little potential to grow, and are likely to lose their chips to those on the larger poker tables.

Vodafone has designed its merger and acquisitions mechanisms to match its prowess at the poker table, resulting in a continuous stream of acquisitions around the globe. Using the power of its share price, Vodafone could obtain the unlimited funding to constantly go for new acquisitions. Access to funding, bidding process, closing the deal, incorporating the new acquisitions into the group management processes (such as financial management and strategy), getting obvious synergies fast (without heavy integration), are the key Cylinder processes that Vodafone has set up to become the dominant player on the global mobile market.

In a second (parallel) Cylinder, Vodafone rolls out the underlying synergies of its acquisitions, such as global procurement, service development, and marketing/branding/distribution strategies.

than taking huge steps, NASA splits its activities into more, smaller missions and learns by repeating the missions. A given mission covers only a portion of the unknown area that will eventually be explored, and so reduces the uncertainty that has been taken on. The programs represent a series of repetitions of almost identical missions, allowing a stepped improvement and a gradual building of knowledge and learning. Another element of stability is that the astronauts are part of the team responsible for a series of missions from the beginning to the end, and the astronauts remain constant throughout that whole series of missions.

For people working within Cylinders, potential feelings of disruption are minimized primarily by maintaining continuity across the cycles. The power structures of the organization are largely maintained, and the most important feedback mechanisms, such as performance measures, are also largely maintained across the cycles. Within a given cycle, power structures and feedback mechanisms are specific to the cycle itself, but they are of secondary, long-term importance. Organizational learning and individual learning are encouraged, to build experience in dealing with the repetitive innovation built into the cycle. So the innovation continues. Substantial efforts are maintained to build and strengthen the culture so that

Professionalism = expertise + new challenges

The individuals who fit particularly well within the Cylinder culture enjoy pushing back frontiers; they believe "knowledge is power." At best Cylinder individuals are deeply informed, yet continuously inquisitive. At worst, Cylinder individuals have blind spots that, when combined with arrogance, become dangerous. The Cylinder individuals' favorite saying? "Practice makes perfect."

CHAPTER 4

The sphere

Finding the most stable route among many possible alternatives

Spheres reduce disruption by developing the maximum number of options for responding to environmental changes. The key words are *assessment* and *action*. Best-practice Spheres are not universally flexible; they can roll any which way but not move up and down. Rather, they are designed to maintain as much flexibility as is needed. Spheres basically play the numbers game, ensuring that they don't miss an opportunity and suffer major disruption as a result. Any potential feelings of disruption are minimized, primarily by stimulating an environment of calculated risk taking.

Best-practice Spheres apply a form of natural selection to find the most stable route forward among the many possible alternatives. Many options are kept open with limited investments, and they are kept open as long as possible to see which bets are most likely to prove profitable. Only then are sizable investments made. Or Spheres might pursue alternate routes that others have created. This approach, and the gambles it entails, creates an ability to survive in very turbulent environments where the future is hard to predict. We're not talking of unlimited flexibility, which would be immensely disruptive. Nor are we suggesting that the Sphere is the optimal structure for all situations. In a low-turbulence environment, the Sphere is not cost efficient. Nor is the Sphere the best structure for coping with known repetitive changes.

The strategy, processes, resources, and organization of a Sphere have to encourage more flexibility than those of any other structure (see Figure 4.1). Strategy focuses very much around propagating a shared vision that can bind people together, even in an unknowable future. Processes tend to be structured around maintaining risk levels within acceptable boundaries, so the company will not be fundamentally damaged. The reward system is based on the "hit rate" of the gambles taken, as well as on maintaining motivation in the face of well-executed

Strategy	• Strategy is reflected in a shared vision that is the glue holding all the people together going on average in the right direction. • The leadership role is to charismatically propagate the vision.
Process	• Planning is based on the end results, not on the intermediate steps. • Control is based on keeping the risk level within boundaries that do not endanger the sustainability of the company. • Financial management is geared to playing the numbers (portfolio investment theory).
Resources	• Personnel selection is based on hiring primarily for attitude and values above skills. • The competencies relating to content (as opposed to process) may vary significantly over time and therefore may be hired in. • Success is perceived as being part of a winning team, and the main motivator for personnel is normally pushing back frontiers. • The reward system is based on the hit rate that you achieve with the experimentational investments and is designed to maintain motivation after well-executed failed attempts.
Organization	• The level of empowerment is high within clear boundaries within which experimentation is allowed. • The roles and functions are fluid. • Training is geared to show people how to get the most out of their initiative. • The values and unwritten rules encourage nonconformist behavior and create heroes from the people who come up with the winning numbers.

Figure 4.1 Best-practice Spheres are not universally flexible.

failures. Empowerment is kept high, within clear boundaries, so the atmosphere is a controlled experiment that never drifts toward anarchy.

A classic example of the Sphere is a typical R&D lab. The lab manages a portfolio of diverse research, exploring which areas look potentially attractive but never knowing in advance which will bear fruit. Pruning becomes appropriate as heavier investments are required. Only toward the end of a particular development program is it possible to trace backward just which original research came through advanced development and eventually produced something good enough to test in the marketplace.

Many Sphere structures can be found among the large companies of Silicon Valley. Cisco Systems, for example, is the leading producer of data communications equipment for Internet applications, and it needs to make sure that it never misses out on, or loses out to, a new technology. Like other Silicon Valley companies, Cisco knows that everything in the Valley moves quickly—Internet protocol, software releases, intelligent agents—and it knows that it can't develop everything itself. So it ventures out and makes its bets, and by doing so wisely provides stability amid turbulence.

Together with major investment banks, Cisco takes stakes in many start-ups, creating a win-win solution and a win-win chance for the future: The small start-ups can try to get their technology to the market and make it successful; if they succeed, Cisco is well placed to bring that technology inside. And Cisco knows what a start-up is like because it was one not so long ago. It integrates only at the last possible moment when a winning technology arises; it waits until the last possible moment to absorb a small company. This strategy allows Cisco to remain stable while constantly adapting. On occasions when Cisco is uncertain which product or service will prevail, it encourages the new product or technology of its venture investment to go to market along-side its own. The market decides the winner.

Sony takes a different approach, leveraging its strong brand name as it plays the numbers game. In the ever-changing global market of consumer audio, video, and PC systems, marketing and product development are subject to rapid, unpredictable change. Sony excels at playing the numbers game: It encourages innovation and brings the results to the market. Sony marketing has learned to react very rapidly and build on its past knowledge.

Within Sony, rebellion and risk taking are rewarded, as long as the Sony brand name is not under fire. There is little hierarchical or peer in-fluence; consensus-based management is not appreciated; it's even hated by top management. A typical story within Sony is that "if everyone agrees something is a good innovation, it must be an ordinary product."

A good example is Sony's entry into the game-station market. Nintendo had asked Sony to develop its next-generation game stations, but the deal fell through. Some enthusiasts at Sony were eager to do it alone, but top management feared that entry into the new market of game playing might dilute the strong brand identity in audio and video. Management also viewed the gaming market as risky and worried that a failure there would tarnish Sony's string of successes. But eventually the gaming enthusiasts prevailed and were proven right: the Sony Playstation established the company as a market leader.

Sony has consistently demonstrated that it can quickly copy successes within itself. Sony applies this very broad approach even though it implies taking risks and *that* means that quite a few of its experiments will fail. Marketers at Sony find stability in the knowledge that a strong Sony brand name will bring winning numbers.

THE VIRTUAL UTILITY: UTILITY.COM

The key impact of e-business on the utility industry is that the different functions of the value chain can be unbundled and performed by different players. The value chain consisted traditionally of the network operator (infrastructure maintenance) and the supply company (service provider). These two companies are now split up into many entities.

Already you see that players start to specialize on specific roles in the value chain and perform them better than the traditional players due to their focus and scale in the activity. For meter reading you see players like Abacus providing instant and continuous meter reading via remote radio/phone signal. For billing you see BBT taking up a role in the value chain. For energy purchasing and customer service you see players like Enermetrix adding value traditionally created by the utility companies. Also many new entrants are taking up positions between the traditional players and the customers/suppliers. E-malls (several utility shops under one), Price comparers, Aggregators (grouping customers to get quantity discounts), Energy auctions and many more are arising.

In this new situation, where every service can be performed better than you can do it yourself, integrators are arising that outsource as many activities as they can and focus on getting sharp deals with all the specialists. Examples of such integrators are Utility.com and Yello Strom that do nothing more than provide the glue between the different providers (Figure 4.2). They act as much as possible as a virtual company.

These integrators act as typical Spheres because they leave all options open by not cornering themselves in specific operations and/or contracts that they sign with the providers. Everybody knows that the mess in the value chain is temporary. Yet no one knows who will eventually dominate the value chain—or how it will be accomplished. It may be the company that "owns" the customer, but it also could very well be the one that has sufficient scale in specific functions. To maximize your chance to win, you need to play the numbers game, and that is what they do by maximizing the amount of bets and minimizing the stakes.

What will the future look like? Nobody knows, but Utility.com and Yello Strom plan to be there. They create stability for their people not by knowing the way forward, but by building a future position based on brand in the marketplace.

For people working within a Sphere, feelings of disruption are minimized primarily by stimulating an environment of calculated risk taking. That requires relatively few formal rules as well as guidelines that allow freedom of action within previously anticipated risk boundaries. Fuzzy, permeable, intraorganizational boundaries allow a free flow of information and personnel. Spheres simply cannot survive if strong silos and boundaries delineate different departments. Nor can Spheres tolerate much hierarchy. To avoid the feelings of disruption that constant evolution may bring, a relatively flat hierarchy with little emphasis on status or centralized control goes a long way. That allows a rapid local evolution rather than a small number of people at the top of the organization deciding how the others ought to be behaving. All

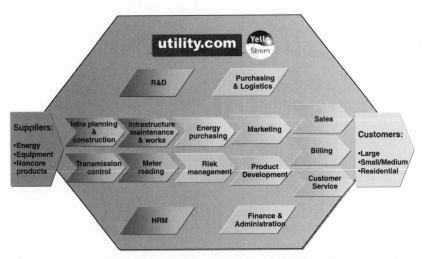

Figure 4.2 Integrators glue different functions together forming virtual companies.

this is strongly reinforced by a vision that provides continuity to the employees. Ultimately, the culture reinforces a risk/reward management model:

Professionalism = flexibility + opportunism

The character trait that is most important within a Sphere is the enjoyment of tackling new challenges; Sphere individuals believe "the journey is the destination." At best, Sphere individuals are incredibly flexible, creative, and innovative. At worst, they can turn into butterflies that cannot or will not consolidate experience. A favorite saying is "you win some, you lose some."

In the following chapters we will demonstrate how you can build the appropriate portfolio of stability structures. We'll start by examining the techniques that each stability structure uses to maximize stability.

CHAPTER 5

Shock absorbers

Techniques based in understanding how people react to change

Maximizing stability, minimizing disruption: the two go hand in hand. In this chapter we want to start by examining the nature of disruption, and then some "shock-absorbing" techniques to minimize it.

Our view is that change feels disruptive to people *only when it is perceived as a significant culture change* for the organization. Why do we say that? Turbulence is not an abstraction; it is something people *feel*. The impact of turbulence, then, is in the minds of people—and that's where we've got to look to distinguish between disruptive and nondisruptive change. Many events that are potentially disruptive at first glance do not actually cause changes to the complex pattern of interpretations that people draw on as they try to work out "how things really work around here"—that is, the unwritten rules of the *culture* in their organization.[1] When this complex pattern is left undisturbed, the events are not disruptive. The start of the annual cycle in a finance department, as we've noted, may be a change, but it's not a disruption. The unwritten rules about how to behave, who's important, how you go about getting the things that are important to you—all these remain the same. Only the dates and the numbers have changed.

On the other hand, when the unwritten rules shift and the culture is disrupted—by a *misfit* or an *overload*—people experience disruption and become susceptible to cumulative change fatigue. By *misfit* we mean a shift in the unwritten rules: if a new pattern of unwritten rules emerges that's less attractive in terms of how well it satisfies personal goals, people will experience a *motivational misfit*. When workers see there's been a change, they calculate how it affects them.

[1]See Peter Scott-Morgan, *The Unwritten Rules of the Game*, McGraw-Hill, 1994.

If, on balance, they find they are worse off, the change feels disruptive. This misfit is a misalignment with what motivates people.

Besides the motivational misfit, people sometimes find themselves in a *conflictual misfit*. Things change and the new interpretations of the pattern of unwritten rules do not fit with the existing pattern of the status quo. Perhaps someone introduces a set of performance measures that simply doesn't fit with the old ones. People now may be encouraged to be entrepreneurial, take risks, and be innovative, when the existing systems they learned to work by require them to play it safe and not change. An internal conflict arises. But it's disruptive for a different reason than when there is motivational misfit.

Motivational and conflictual misfits can arise immediately or they can build over time. A misfit may be *instant:* "People have changed the performance measures and I'm going to be worse off," or "People have changed the organization structure and now a no-win is built into the system." People sense the conflict immediately, and the disruption is immediate. A more difficult situation is a *progressive* misfit, when either the motivational or conflictual misfit builds over time through a series of gradual changes in the pattern of unwritten rules. The system drifts away from satisfying personal goals as well as the original did or it creates increasingly apparent internal conflict.

Although motivational and conflictual misfits represent the majority of perceived disruptions in an organization, another source of perceived disruption comes from simple *overload*. The pattern changes too dramatically, too often, or stretches out over too long a time period. The constant need to work out the implications of the new patterns becomes tiring. That occurs even if the new patterns are all as attractive as the past. It's just like when someone gets married, changes his or her job, moves to a new country, and plans to build a dream house. Each of these is a positive, yet they add up to an overload. Brains grow exhausted from constantly having to process the new patterns.

As we can see in Figure 5.1, the lower the level of misfit, the higher the overload that can be tolerated and vice versa. If the level of misfit

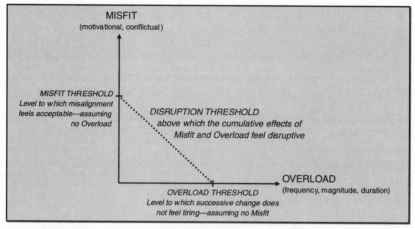

Figure 5.1 People do perceive disruption (and therefore become susceptible to cumulative change fatigue) if there is too much misfit or overload.

is low, people can tolerate more, faster, and heavier change without crossing the overload threshold. If the overload threshold is high because of frequent, large, or long sets of changes, people can tolerate only a relatively low amount of discordance built into the system before they cross the disruption threshold. As we separate these different forms of potential disruption to understand them, we must note that they all coexist in someone's mind. Only by assessing the cumulative total effect can we determine the disruption experienced and whether people can easily accommodate the changes involved. Only after the change crosses a threshold and threatens change fatigue does it become a full-fledged disruption (Figure 5.2).

Although we've looked at different reasons why something can be perceived as disruptive, it's useful to have a simple test for disruption and the turbulence that causes it. We call this the *Hibernation test.* Imagine that you put someone from a particular part of the business into deep-freeze suspended animation before an event starts. When the event is finished, you thaw that person out and ask yourself if he or she still knows all the correct unwritten rules. Would that person know how to behave? Would the culture feel the same? If the answer is

Instant motivational Misfit	"I joined to do pure research, not glorified development work!"
Progressive motivational Misfit	"I can't tell you when it started, but I'm finding myself less and less satisfied by the job...."
Instant conflictual Misfit	"We're all supposed to be team players—but ultimately I've got to stand out if I'm going to get promoted."
Progressive conflictual Misfit	"Why doesn't anyone bother with turning to the monthly debriefs anymore?"
Frequency Overload	"What were we supposed to do? I can't keep up anymore...."
Magnitude Overload	"I'm swamped! It's all become too much and too complex."
Duration Overload	"I feel ridiculous. Everything's so great, and there's not really been anything you could call stressful, but for some reason I just feel tired all the time!"

Figure 5.2 Examples of symptoms caused by crossing the disruption threshold.

yes, the event was not disruptive. Because the unwritten rules have remained the same, there was no underlying turbulence.

Let's try the Hibernation test for the accounts department of a company. On December 31 we put somebody into deep freeze. We thaw that person out a few days later, after the annual cycle has started anew. We anticipate that when the person is thawed out, he or she will still know the sensible way to behave. The people he or she is working with are the same, the processes this person is following are the same, the advice he or she would give a friend in the department about how to behave is the same. Our conclusion: we've had a change but no disruption—and no turbulence.

So what exactly drives the unwritten rules of the organization, and how can we focus on what specifically must not change if we are to avoid disruption? The culture is determined by three main drivers: Motivators, Enablers, and Triggers.

Motivators are generally not affected by external events. They correspond to what is important to you, what gets you up in the morning, what it is that you really value as part of your job. Equally important is what you want to avoid. What penalties do you not want to incur? Motivators are deep seated and fundamental to individuals and tend to be quite common to the individuals within a given organization. They correspond to things like exciting work, respect, belonging to a group, and taking pride in an organization, as well as money earned.

Enablers and Triggers are the drivers that represent the means of achieving what is important to you. Enablers are almost an unwritten organization chart, corresponding to who is important and how you should act toward them. Linking Motivators and Enablers are the Triggers. These are frequently the formal and informal performance measures of an organization. Triggers correspond to the timing of important events and therefore to how you should act.

So we have a triad of drivers:

- *Motivators:* what is important to you.
- *Enablers:* who is important to you because he or she can grant or withhold that Motivator.
- *Triggers:* what the Enabler will look at to decide whether you get what is important to you.

The combination of Motivators, Enablers, and Triggers drives the complex pattern of unwritten rules within an organization. As we've seen, too great a change in that pattern of unwritten rules, or disconnects in the pattern of unwritten rules, creates perceived turbulence.

Other factors, of course, can influence the unwritten rules, including national and local culture, economic climate, private agendas, and so on. But these are beyond management's influence, so let's be rigorously pragmatic. To minimize the perceived disruption within an organization, we must focus only on what we can influence—the Enablers and the Triggers, that is, the power structure and the feedback systems within the organization. Over the years of studying unwritten rules we've seen that misfit, both motivational and conflictual, is directly attributable to misalignment of Motivators, Enablers, and Triggers (Figure 5.3).

In each example in Figure 5.3, the top heading represents the misfit. The bottom capitalized heading represents the resultant cumulative change fatigue that can build up if the misfit is more than just an isolated instance. As Figure 5.3 shows, the question is not just whether the misfit is with Motivators, Enablers, and Triggers, but also how strongly the misfit is being pushed relative to the status quo.

Because Motivators are tied to what is important to individuals and their values, they are generally not affected by external events. Although an individual's Motivators evolve over time, they remain remarkably constant. What is important to people when they're children evolves as they grow into teenagers and evolves again as they reach adulthood. Dealing with groups of individuals within an organization, the common denominator of Motivators corresponds to the core values of the organization, and, as a result, they are largely immutable. They are necessarily strongly reinforced by management systems and management actions. They also tend to be self-fulfilling because of the recruitment process: if you don't share broadly the same Motivators as other people in the organization, you suffer the corporate equivalent of a tissue rejection. You

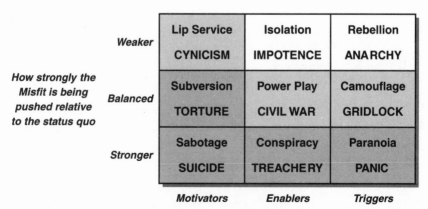

		Motivators	Enablers	Triggers
How strongly the Misfit is being pushed relative to the status quo	Weaker	Lip Service / CYNICISM	Isolation / IMPOTENCE	Rebellion / ANARCHY
	Balanced	Subversion / TORTURE	Power Play / CIVIL WAR	Camouflage / GRIDLOCK
	Stronger	Sabotage / SUICIDE	Conspiracy / TREACHERY	Paranoia / PANIC

Figure 5.3 Misfit—both motivational and conflictual—is directly attributable to misalignment of Motivators, Enablers, and Triggers.

don't enjoy being with those other people; they don't enjoy being around you. Within a year, you are glad to leave and your colleagues are glad to see you go.

Even under duress and extreme pressure, people do not change what is fundamentally important to them. So for all these reasons, we can assume that the Motivators will not be significantly affected by external events and pressures that are causing the potential disruption within the organization. Rather, it's the cumulative changes of Enablers and Triggers that cause change fatigue.

How, then, can we minimize the shocks to Enablers and Triggers? Through three shock-absorbing techniques:

- *Bridging* provides continuity by maintaining select Enablers and Triggers that span potentially disruptive events.

- *Creeping* absorbs minor potential turbulence into a gradual drift of rigorously aligned Enablers and Triggers.

- *Surging* smoothes major potential turbulence by accelerating aligned shifts of Enablers and Triggers to the maximum nondisruptive levels.

In the coming chapters, we'll look at each in turn.

CHAPTER 6

Bridging and Creeping

Providing continuity from one side of change to the other

Imagine a company redesigning its remuneration system, perhaps with the advice of external consultants. At the beginning of the initiative, the company stresses the continuity of the status quo and communicates that the existing formal organizational structure will remain in place. Or, to use our terminology, the Enablers remain fundamentally the same (although the influence of the consultants may informally be added, at least while the consultants are still around). At the beginning of the process, the existing performance measures (the Triggers) remain unchanged. The recommendations that come from the redesign of the remuneration system will be geared toward reflecting the current culture, so they will fit the organization and the aspirations of its people as well as possible. As a result, if the remuneration system is redesigned in a smart way, many Enablers and Triggers will be maintained. New Triggers, and occasionally new Enablers, will be tied into the old system. Indeed, that system will be designed so the Motivators are still satisfied or, better yet, even more satisfied than in the past.

Such a process is an example of the classic *Bridging* technique, that is, providing continuity within the organization by maintaining specified Enablers and Triggers on either side of a potentially disruptive event (Figure 6.1). Of course, there have been many change initiatives in which the designers have not attempted to maximize Bridging—especially when they have *wanted* to shake up the organization. These initiatives have often been criticized for "throwing the baby out with the bath water"; they have tended to lead to unnecessary change fatigue. Bridging has a lot to offer.

To make Bridging work, as many Enablers and Triggers as possible should be retained after the event, and they must remain rigorously aligned. New Enablers and Triggers need to be aligned with the orig-

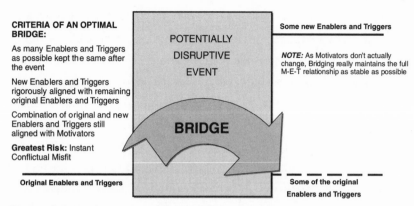

Figure 6.1 Bridging provides continuity by maintaining select Enablers and Triggers that span potentially disruptive events.

inal Enablers and Triggers. And all Enablers and Triggers need to remain aligned with Motivators.

The great risk of a Bridge is that, if you haven't thought through the potential disconnects, some new Enablers and Triggers do not fit with the original ones. In practice, as Motivators don't tend to change, Bridging really is about maintaining stability in the Motivator-Enabler-Trigger relationship. While the focus is on Enablers and Triggers, the outcome is to keep in place as many unwritten rules as possible. Disruption only occurs if there is too much change in those unwritten rules.

Creeping absorbs potential turbulence into a gradual drift of rigorously aligned Enablers and Triggers. Imagine a TQM initiative on the factory floor. The existing processes are carefully designed so they are internally consistent. There's likely to be a quality circle with a flat hierarchy that results in many balanced Enablers. Statistical Process Control (SPC) may be used to monitor performance (providing a consistent Trigger), and there is an overarching vision of continuous improvement. The purpose of TQM is not to keep things the same, of course, but to evolve gradually. So the root causes of minor disruptions are analyzed and improvements are agreed upon. The quality circle implicitly ensures that the improvements are fully aligned with the existing processes. The Enablers and Triggers remain constant, and the quality circles tend to be put together with members selected for their inside knowledge and cutting-edge expertise. These people will appreciate the implications of making changes and can ensure alignment and consistency with existing processes. SPC and other Triggers encourage long-term conformity with the quality vision, so Creeping occurs as a gradual shift. Throughout the Creep, the Enablers and Triggers remain rigorously aligned with each other and with the Motivators (Figure 6.2).

Creep maintains old Enablers and Triggers as they gradually evolve into new Enablers and Triggers. In an optimal Creep, Enablers and Triggers are rigorously aligned; in practice, low levels of misfit are common and acceptable, provided they remain below the misfit threshold. Should the Enablers and Triggers get slightly out of alignment, no disruption need occur because most organizations can tolerate some modest level of disconnect. A larger misalignment, however, creates the risk that Creeping will produce a progressive

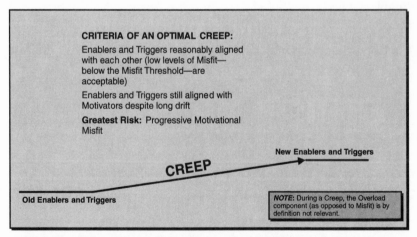

Figure 6.2 Creeping absorbs minor potential turbulence into a gradual drift of rigorously aligned Enablers and Triggers.

motivational misfit: the Enablers and Triggers may remain reasonably aligned but the benefits they bring start shifting away from the benefits that individuals are looking for.

During a Creep, the overload component (as opposed to the misfit) is, by definition, irrelevant; the progression and evolution of Enablers and Triggers can never be so high that overload becomes an issue. When the rate of migration is sufficiently high that potential overload is a consideration, we move to the third potential shock-absorbing technique—Surging.

CHAPTER 7

Surging

Going to the brink of disruption

Surging smoothes major potential turbulence by accelerating aligned shifts of Enablers and Triggers to the maximum level that individuals will not find disruptive. The key to a successful Surge is to focus enough on the risk of disruption to allow the transition to be as fast, as long, and as dramatic as possible without the risk of change fatigue. A Surge is much more than a fast Creep, and management attention has to be focused on areas of potential disruption.

Imagine the postacquisition integration of a company. When the integration is done well, a large amount of effort is spent on two-way communication. The rationale of the integration and the anticipated benefit is communicated in one direction. In the other direction a communication channel needs to be open for people to present their concerns and the problems they encounter. In other words, an understanding is needed of the Motivators, Enablers, and Triggers of the acquired personnel to ensure there's no misfit and to ensure a lowering of the barriers to change.

A second benefit of a successful integration is the newly acquired company can maintain, at least initially, a certain autonomy (as in IBM's acquisition of Lotus Development). In this case, a reduced pace of change reduces the risk of frequency overload and conflictual misfit. Semiautonomy also provides opportunities to explore approaches to integration and to develop a shared vision. That, in turn, helps pull the Surge forward, so that top management doesn't have to push aggressively from behind. Finally, the successful integration depends on constantly testing for and trying to understand growing problems in order to avoid crossing the disruption threshold.

Surge is sometimes implicitly accomplished in change-management programs that take rigorous account of human factors. Indeed, an analysis of many successful changes demonstrates that without using the terminology and the models we've described, the Surge has nevertheless followed the criteria suggested.

Those criteria ensure that the Surge is not so dramatic or so fast that the new patterns exhaust the people involved (Figure 7.1). They also ensure that the Enablers and Triggers are aligned with each other as rigorously as possible, even though the rate of change can make that quite difficult. As in all other cases, Enablers and Triggers need to be maintained in alignment with what's important to people—Motivators. Without a doubt the greatest risk in Surge is that overload may lead to a disruptive, wrenching change, just like the Lewin changes of the past.

Don't make the mistake of thinking a Surge can be achieved simply by accelerating an evolutionary change. In practice, an optimal surge can be achieved only by trying to move to the limit and then pulling back a bit—just as a Grand Prix driver must push to the limit, risk an occasional skid, then back off on the throttle and regain control. To Surge, push things to the maximum, but pay sharp attention to the divide between being at the limit and breaking into a disruptive, fatiguing Lewin-style change. In a Surge, both overload and misfit components are critical,

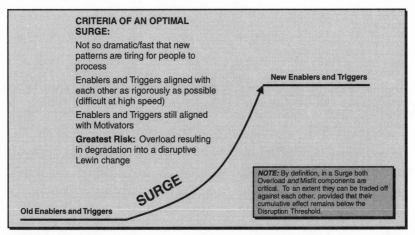

Figure 7.1 Surging smoothes major potential turbulence by accelerating aligned shifts of Enablers and Triggers to the maximum nondisruptive levels.

although to a certain extent they can be traded off against each other so long as their cumulative effect remains below the disruption threshold.

For an optimal Surge, management focus is critical in at least five areas:

- Consider the potential braking forces that individuals' concerns may create.
- Use a cascaded visioning technique to pull the Surge forward.
- Use communications and training to support the Surge.
- Create and maintain a "Surge group" that can anticipate and manage potential misalignments.
- Test constantly for early signs of hot spots and take action as needed.

A failure on any of these fronts can turn the Surge into a Lewin change. Let's look at each in turn.

Individuals' Concerns. The Surge should be designed and managed to minimize the potential braking forces of individuals' concerns. Each person encouraged to progress through the Surge needs to be able to answer positively these questions:

1. Is change necessary?
2. Is the proposed change appropriate?
3. Can I give up the past?
4. Do I have the skills and resources required?
5. Does the formal/informal system support the required changes?

Only if all five are answered positively by the vast majority of those involved will the brakes be off. Generally, in the early stages of the Surge, focus on the "thought leaders" of the organization, those people who, if they change their minds, tend to change others' minds as well. If those thought leaders come aboard, they can pull the rest through the Surge.

Cascading Vision Techniques. The easiest way to develop shared visions is to create a set of emotional magnets within the organization. A successful vision needs to contain at least three components: aspiration, inspiration, and perspiration. *Aspiration* is about what the new organization will look like. If that's specified only in numerical terms, the majority of people won't embrace the vision passionately. *Inspiration* gets people excited about the goal they're heading toward. *Perspiration* is the work to be done, highlighting the mechanism by which people can make the trade-offs needed to achieve the vision.

It's very difficult to find one overarching vision that pulls everyone within a particular department or division in the same direction. So the most practical way of encouraging a Surge is to build a cascade of visions. The highest vision may be within the particular part of the organization going through the Surge; supplementary visions at the team level and a series of personal visions that tie into the overall vision lead everyone through the Surge.

Communication and Training. Communication of the goals of the Surge starts at the top. You need to reinforce the desire to do even better when things are going well, to send reassurance that the disruption will be minimal, and to signal what the new Enablers and Triggers are. Bottom-up communication is just as important, so top management learns quickly of the disconnects appearing within the Enablers-and-Triggers framework. Managers need to sense where change fatigue is developing. They need suggestions from those involved at the day-to-day cutting edge of change so they can see what mechanisms will avoid the change fatigue should the Surge cross the disruption threshold.

It's also essential to focus on just-in-time and task-aligned training to encourage those within the Surge to feel that they have the competencies needed for the new behaviors required. This requires a combination of classroom teaching and training in new skills and techniques and the transfer of a lot of tacit, hidden knowledge that can only be accomplished through coaching.

A Surge Group. This underused technique is ideal for maintaining an optimal surge. Have representatives from various teams, maybe even from other parts of the business, come together as a group whose sole responsibility is to sit down regularly—perhaps even daily for as little as 15 minutes—to discuss what potential disruption may be developing within their organizations. The representative of team A describes what team A is doing that might have implications for the Enablers and Triggers of team B, team C, and so forth. Similarly, the representative from team C discusses the implications of changes to the Enablers and Triggers that will affect the other parts of the organization. It's a way of avoiding unanticipated disruption caused by the complexity of trying to move so fast and so broadly up a Surge.

Test Constantly for Hot Spots. Common testing techniques include spontaneous interviews to check for developing misalignments, maintaining a "what's wrong?" hotline that people can call anonymously and running quick-and-dirty unwritten rules appraisals by focus groups that test what the current Enablers and Triggers are. These techniques are a quick means of ensuring that what is perceived as the current set of unwritten rules corresponds to what people recognize in their day-to-day lives. This can be supplemented by circulating the results of a full unwritten rules appraisal, asking people whether they recognize any changes to "what feels like the sensible way to behave."

CHAPTER 8

Matching shock absorbers to the structures

Each stability structure uses all the techniques, but to different degrees

When we put together our three shock-absorbing techniques—Bridging, Creeping, and Surging—with our four stability structures—Pyramid, Cylinder, Cube, and Sphere—we find that each structure applies the techniques in different ways. Pyramids specialize in Bridging techniques and Cubes in Surging techniques. Cylinders are all-rounders, balancing Bridging, Creeping, and Surging techniques. Spheres specialize in a uniquely interlaced Creeping and Surging technique. In each case, whatever the stability structure, these consistent principles apply:

- Always *Bridge* as much as possible, at a level above the potential disruption of the event.
- *Creep* as needed unless the end goal is too far off to be reached in time.
- *Surge* when Creep is not sufficient.

Each stability structure uses all the techniques, *but to different degrees* (Figure 8.1). Let's examine each structure in turn.

Pyramids. Successful Pyramids keep many of their performance measures and much of their organization structure stable over time (Bridging) (Figure 8.2). As a result of this, incremental change with a long-term view is natural and people in Pyramids tend to have long-term career expectations within the company. Hand in hand with that is often a difficulty in adopting revolutionary changes. This helps explain why Creep was adopted so successfully by large pyramidal organizations in Japan, while Business Process Reengineering, which required a major overhaul and a rethinking of how the organization should be operating, often created havoc. We can also see why Pyramids choose to set up parallel structures, as IBM did with its

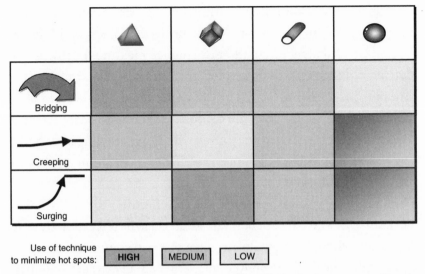

Use of technique to minimize hot spots: **HIGH** MEDIUM LOW

Figure 8.1 Each stability structure applies the techniques according to consistent principles.

skunkworks, GM with Saturn, and P&G with Reflect.com. The Bridging that made them such good Pyramids precluded them from taking a radical step within the existing Pyramid. However, that same Bridging diminished their ability to absorb the lessons of the radically new approaches back into the parent company.

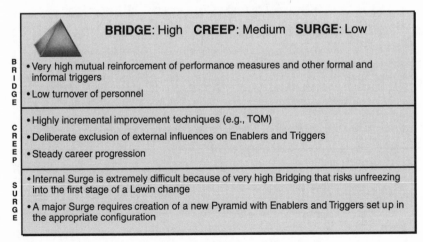

BRIDGE: High **CREEP**: Medium **SURGE**: Low

BRIDGE
- Very high mutual reinforcement of performance measures and other formal and informal triggers
- Low turnover of personnel

CREEP
- Highly incremental improvement techniques (e.g., TQM)
- Deliberate exclusion of external influences on Enablers and Triggers
- Steady career progression

SURGE
- Internal Surge is extremely difficult because of very high Bridging that risks unfreezing into the first stage of a Lewin change
- A major Surge requires creation of a new Pyramid with Enablers and Triggers set up in the appropriate configuration

Figure 8.2 Pyramids specialize in Bridging techniques.

Cubes. Throughout history, armies worldwide have relied heavily on training and on shared values. The Bridged Enablers and Triggers (organizational structure and performance measures) provide the glue to hold the periodic Surges together and keep the army bonded through the drama of war. They also provide the ability to shift rapidly and efficiently from the consolidation phase (peace time) to the transition phase (war time). Only with heavy training and shared core values can armies accomplish so efficiently the dramatic Surges required of them (Figure 8.3).

Similarly, NASA was able to rapidly and effectively cope with potential disaster, as when the Apollo 13 mission had to be rescued en route to the Moon—the most dramatic problem that had confronted the space agency since the fatal fire on Apollo 1. This was an extreme, unanticipated Surge, but NASA was ready because it was geared up in Cube form. NASA was able to maintain the massively complex infrastructure needed for a successful mission because the key Enablers and the key Triggers were already Bridged. Despite the extraordinary adaptation required within only a few days, the core power structure and the core performance measures remained the same. Consequently, the organiza-

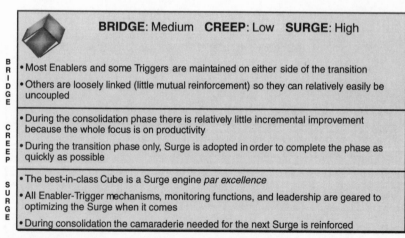

	BRIDGE: Medium **CREEP**: Low **SURGE**: High
B R I D G E	• Most Enablers and some Triggers are maintained on either side of the transition • Others are loosely linked (little mutual reinforcement) so they can relatively easily be uncoupled
C R E E P	• During the consolidation phase there is relatively little incremental improvement because the whole focus is on productivity • During the transition phase only, Surge is adopted in order to complete the phase as quickly as possible
S U R G E	• The best-in-class Cube is a Surge engine *par excellence* • All Enabler-Trigger mechanisms, monitoring functions, and leadership are geared to optimizing the Surge when it comes • During consolidation the camaraderie needed for the next Surge is reinforced

Figure 8.3 Cubes specialize in Surging techniques.

tion was able to Surge into an unanticipated radically different form, hold together and find triumph at the brink of disaster.

Cylinders. The client projects of international consulting companies around the world are good illustrations of why Cylinders are all-rounders, balancing Bridging, Creeping, and Surging techniques (Figure 8.4).

They're organized to minimize the disruption caused by project hopping. People within international consulting companies are changing (sometimes month to month) from one organizational structure to another. The day-to-day boss is the project leader but only for the duration of the assignment so the project leader is a temporary Enabler within a given project cycle. A consultant's career, however, is managed by a coach. In other words, one key Enabler is Bridged across the cycles.

Consultants are measured primarily on sales and billability (the percentage of available time the consultant is billing a client). Those performance measures—Triggers—are Bridged across the cycles; they're not unique to any particular project in which the consultant is involved.

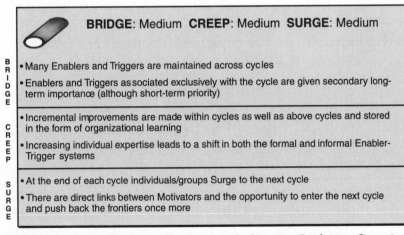

Figure 8.4 Cylinders are all-rounders balancing Bridging, Creeping, and Surging techniques.

Knowledge management is critical if lessons are to be learned on projects and leveraged across the whole organization. The knowledge management allows Creep for the whole consulting company, gradually evolving as organizational learning embedded across the organization. Over the first 5 to 10 years a consultant is expected to become progressively more effective, and is rewarded accordingly. It's a gradual evolution, a Creep.

At the start of each assignment a project team rapidly assimilates a new client, a new project leader, a new goal, a new organizational structure. A series of changes that in many other organizations would be massively disruptive becomes nothing more than business as usual because of the way the changes are managed and because the project team is used to going through this form of Surge. Extensive training and standardization in work methods and writing and working styles help to minimize the Surge of each new team. People who have never seen or worked with each other before may be coming together with a client that they've never known before, but the common denominator of techniques, methods, procedures, and styles in which they will be operating is sufficient to reassure all involved.

Spheres. When we look at the ways in which Spheres specialize in interlaced Creeping and Surging techniques, we start to understand why current best practices for innovation and creativity advocate minimal rules, shared vision, permeable boundaries, and effective communications (Figure 8.5).

These attributes, commonly recognized as best practice for learning organizations are, in our terminology, light-to-minimal Bridging. If significant Bridging is not providing the glue, something else is needed to forestall the breakup of the organization. That something is *reinforced shared Motivators:* a common shared passion that is the aim of the Spherer. Research-based organizations, such as pharmaceutical companies, manage a portfolio of projects but keep refocusing on areas that prove fruitful. That makes tremendous sense when we understand how a Sphere is supposed to operate. There's very little Bridging; there's a high level of autonomy among the company's different projects. There's

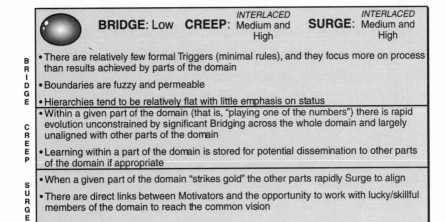

Figure 8.5 Spheres specialize in using interlaced Creeping and Surging techniques.

Creep within the projects, as each group aggressively pursues the avenues of its particular research, and then a Surge across the projects as the company refocuses its portfolio on exciting areas.

By applying various combinations of the shock-absorbing techniques according to consistent principles, each stability structure minimizes the changes to Enablers and Triggers. As a result, the structures minimize the cumulative effects that can create change fatigue. That, in itself, would be sufficient if it were possible to split an organization neatly into stability structures, corresponding to particular innovation patterns. In practice, of course, any part of an organization is likely to deal with various forms of innovation, even if one form is dominant. Generally, a given stability structure can absorb limited amounts of other forms of turbulence than it was designed to accommodate.

Cubes, Cylinders, and Spheres can minimize the disruption of infrequent but known turbulence—that turbulence that would classically be addressed by a Pyramid—by applying an incremental approach on top of whatever shock-absorption techniques they typically use. A Cube can add a bit of Creep into its transition or between transitions in order to absorb the disruption. For instance, during peace time—between "rolls" of the Cube—an army trains its recruits to use new technologies at the same time as it maintains operational performance of existing equipment. In contrast, during the Apollo moonshot program, NASA regularly incorporated the latest evolutions in electronics into each *new* project—during the Surge, as the Cube rolled—but not *during* a project.

The Cylinder can build the Creep into its existing cycles and above the existing cycles. So a consulting company keeps its peoples' expertise current both by on-the-job training at client sites as well as by annual off-site training. The Sphere can add a small amount of Creep to the existing Creeps and Surges it undergoes—as with the researchers in an R&D lab who use scientific journals to update their knowledge of progress in a given field by either tracking articles relating to their current research topic (Creep phase) or reading new journals cover to cover when they pick up a new research topic (Surge phase).

So, absorbing the forms of disruption that a Pyramid would typically address is relatively straightforward (Figure 8.6). Conceptually, you're just adding a bit of incremental Creep on top of whatever else you would be doing.

Absorbing disruption of infrequent, but new turbulence—the sort of situations where a Cube would be the natural structure—is also relatively straightforward. Conceptually, the way to absorb and minimize the disruption of Cubic turbulence is by minimizing the uncertainty of the impact on the Enablers and Triggers structure. Pyramids, Spheres, and Cylinders can all bring in expertise in advance to provide the required level of innovation that's going to be needed, as well as to plan an incremental path. Much of the growth in demand for management consulting has been spurred by companies' desire for help in tackling topics they do not expect to need to address again—meaning they cannot justify building in-house skills. Each Pyramid, Cylinder, and Sphere also has specific compensation techniques (see Figure 8.6) that build upon the shock-absorption techniques in which they specialize.

Pyramids, Cubes, and Spheres can minimize the disruption of frequent, known turbulence—Cylindrical turbulence—by applying the

Structure	Problem in shock absorbing	Compensation technique
△ ⬭ ⬤	• Problems with major Surges	• Hires experts a long way upfront to try to reduce the required level of innovation and to plan as incremental a path as possible • Reduces the uncertainty from inexperience by high intensive application of stability tools
△	• Almost total lack of ability to perform a Surge	• Tries out a Surge technique, but will have great difficulty not letting it break into a Lewin change (so will need to set up a parallel structure)
⬭	• Underdeveloped "big-Surge" capability	• Absorbs the shock by integrating small adaptations for this infrequent, unknown turbulence into a series of existing Surges at the end/ beginning of the cycles
⬤	• Underdeveloped "big-Surge" capability	• Will be spread out and handled as all the frequent, unknown turbulences—perceived as an integral part of one or more of the existing Surges

Figure 8.6 Limited Cubic disruption can be absorbed by each stability structure.

shock absorbers they have in as forceful a way as they know. Pyramids use the Bridging in which they excel to maintain as much stability as possible (for instance, the sales network of an international consumer giant remaining constant despite the fluctuations of seasonal buying). Cubes have to adopt a different technique because the frequency of disruption is much higher than the Cube was designed to accommodate. The key here is to cluster the disruptions into occasional spasmodic innovation and then apply Creep or Surge techniques to accommodate the disruption. So, for example, nonurgent specification changes arising from annual product reviews of the Mark 2 Turboencabulator may be saved up until the Mark 3 is launched a few years later. Finally, Spheres have to try to build some Cylindrical techniques into the Sphere (for instance, annual budgeting for lab equipment). This tends to result in an inefficient form of Cylinder that's incorporated within the Sphere but is nevertheless able to minimize the Cylindrical disruption.

Absorbing frequent, new turbulence—Spherical turbulence—into Pyramids, Cubes, and Cylinders is a more difficult challenge. Pyramids have great difficulty in accepting the frequency and the level of innovation required to cope with Spherical turbulence and under such circumstances suffer more than any other structure. Cubes can apply a technique similar to that used in absorbing Cylindrical turbulence, finding creative ways to cluster the turbulence into the Surges they are conducting anyway—much as politicians gather up unaddressed issues throughout their time in office and turn them into their reelection campaign platform. Put another way, the Cube lowers the frequency of the turbulence and then incorporates it as business as usual. The Cylinder tends to have a bit too much Bridging to absorb the Spherical turbulence and so will have to relax that Bridging for a specific set of cycles and create the equivalent of a "mini-Sphere" within the Cylinder (like the small team of Mr. Fix-Its within a film crew on location). So all but the Pyramid can absorb limited Spherical turbulence.

The three other structures have one more way of coping with Spherical disruption. They can simply split off the Sphere. For example, the marketing communications function is typically a Pyramid that produces the standard media of the company. Imagine, however, that one unit keeps coming up with wild and creative ideas to support the positioning and to react to external events. That unit has a different Enabler—an internal client—for every idea and is playing a numbers game because there are many bad ideas and few brilliant ones to run with. That part of marketing can, and probably should, be outsourced because otherwise it will provide ideas only on request and won't be fast or flexible enough. The innovative positioning part of the business should be set up close to management, which can measure the number of good ideas instead of just having internal clients assessing what is required. In this way what might be a severe Spherical turbulence of potentially great disruption gets outsourced. Conceptually, a separate Sphere is set up that can deal with the highly frequent turbulence that otherwise would result in a buildup of change fatigue within the main organization.

CHAPTER 9

Your collection of structures

Some structures warp but retain their integrity

On the one hand, great reassurance can be found in the knowledge that a given part of an organization needs to know only its dominant innovation pattern to be able to select the appropriate stability structure, confident that it can cope with a certain amount of warping of its main structure. On the other hand, bear in mind that there are limits to this adaptability. The warping of the main structure can only go so far before it becomes unacceptable to those within. We'll return to this later in the book, as we consider the approaches to migrating from one structure to another. At this stage, it's enough to know just how many warped structures are practical.

Over the years we've observed many structures that, when analyzed, were seen to be "warped." Of course, that's exactly what you'd expect given that few were ever designed according to the precepts highlighted in this book. However, what was less expected was that of the basic 12 theoretically possible warped structures—that is, a dominant stability structure with some of the characteristics of one other structure—less than half were attractive to use.

Of the 12 theoretical warped structures, only 5 (e.g., Sphere with a bit of Pyramid) proved stable in the sense that they were relatively easy to maintain in their warped form (Figure 9.1). Four other warped structures (e.g., Cylinder with a bit of Cube) were difficult to maintain because it took a lot of effort to stop the dominant structure from dominating entirely. As a result, they sucked up management time and required a major commitment for the long term. The three remaining apparently possible warped structures proved in reality to be impractical (e.g., Pyramid with a little Sphere) because the secondary characteristics were incompatible with the dominant ones.

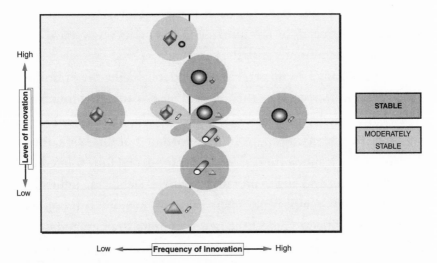

High

Low

Level of Innovation

STABLE

MODERATELY
STABLE

Low ◄———— Frequency of Innovation ————► High

Figure 9.1 There are only five stable and four moderately stable warped structures.

TOM, DICK, AND HARRY—1

For 3 years an ailing international computer services firm had undergone several pendulum swings in strategy. Now, under new leadership, it was finally consolidating around a bold turn-around. But the organization was beginning to show signs of change fatigue—especially from overload.

Tom and Dick, two members of the team responsible for catalyzing the transformation of the company, were meeting with Harry, the VP of training. They had decided that the training function was potentially a critical means of aligning the company with the new strategy and encouraging an overall transformation. Given the nature of the business, everyone went through at least a few days training every 6 months, so the training department had good access to employees at all levels. What's more, with all the uncertainty and turbulence within the organization, the biannual training was one of the few things left that employees perceived as representing continuity with the past.

The Change Managers wanted to persuade the training department to recognize the importance of providing much of the "glue" needed to stop the currently highly turbulent organization from breaking apart. In the shorthand of this book, they believed the training process was a Pyramid, and they wanted to strengthen its Bridging to provide a powerful stabilizing influence to the whole organization. Their proposal was that training be slightly modified to reflect the new corporate strategy, and then frozen in style, location, faculty, and content for 2 years to symbolize and reinforce a feeling of continuity and stability despite all the other changes.

The VP of training refused. He explained that once a year all training underwent an (sometimes major) overhaul. Without doing so, the training would rapidly be perceived as out of date, and he would rightly be out of a job. Training, he insisted, was a Cylinder with a vital Surge every year. As an example of the pressure he was under Harry cited e-business, which was currently a small department within the computer services firm, but one that was growing fast. No one knew, he explained, what its impact would be on the company as a whole, but everyone was telling him that within a few years e-business was likely to affect how the whole company served its clients *and therefore how the whole company had to be trained.* In such an environment, he insisted, it would be unprofessional for him to slow down the rate of change in the training program. On the contrary, he needed to step up the rate. "What's more," Harry added, "now that I think about it, future changes are going not only to be faster but much more uncertain. The training Cylinder should *never* be a Pyramid in this environment—I need to change it to a Sphere!" Voices were raised on both sides . . .

Figure 9.2 is based on observation of (usually) unintentionally warped structures. It lays out a broad sequencing from the Cylinder-Pyramid, where a dominant Cylinder with a bit of Pyramidal behavior proves very easy to maintain, through to the Pyramid-Sphere, which, in practice, is impossible to maintain.

Consider why the sequence is as it is. If you're working within a Cylinder, dealing with repeating cycles, it is relatively easy to maintain some aspects of long-term stability—very little repetition, incremental improvement and relatively high bridging, the Pyramidal characteristics warping the basic Cylinder structure. At the other end of the spectrum, it is conceptually almost impossible to imagine a situation where you had a best-in-class Pyramid that had very heavy Bridging (making it impossible to have rapid Surging), yet nevertheless was capable of absorbing the high-frequency, highly innovative turbulence required for the Sphere.

The limited tolerance of stability structures in warped forms suggests that the best guideline in organizing a company is to maintain

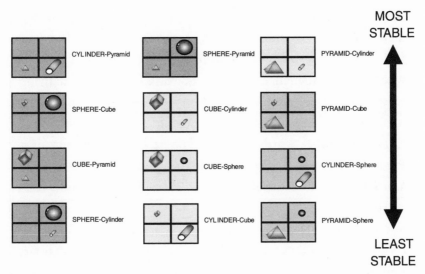

Figure 9.2 Broad sequencing from Cylinder-Pyramid to the Pyramid-Sphere.

TOM, DICK, AND HARRY—2

"You need a lot of Pyramid and I need more and more Sphere," said Harry after his blood pressure had subsided. "Can't we have a *warped* structure that combines both?"

He looked at Figure 9.1 and was initially excited that indeed there was a stable structure linking the upper-right and lower-left quadrants. A Sphere-Pyramid. But his enthusiasm was short lived. "Wait a moment," said Tom. "Isn't that structure too close to the center of the matrix?" Harry looked blank, so the Change Manager continued. "I mean, it's still got a rather high frequency and high level of innovation. And anyway, the Sphere dominates, whereas the bulk of what you do would have to be Pyramidal. . . ."

"What does that mean in English?" Harry's blood pressure was clearly rising again, so Tom's colleague, Dick, raised a calming hand and took over.

"Look, the idea of a warped structure may be a good one, but if we make training a Sphere that is warped in the direction of a Pyramid, then everyone may be unhappy. Think what the words mean. A Sphere is meant for an environment that's fast and furious. I know e-business training may be like that, but most of what your department does is *not*. So you'd probably actually be frustrated if the Sphere was the dominant style of your department. And you can only get away with adding a small amount of rigidity (in other words warp the Sphere in the direction of a Pyramid) before you begin to stifle the creativity of the Sphere. You'd end up with a department that was jack-of-all-training but master of none!"

"Mmmm," Harry conceded, "then are you suggesting we create a warped Pyramid-Sphere, where the Pyramid form dominates?"

"Unfortunately, that's not even an option. Look back at the chart. There is no such stable form. A Pyramid can't be warped enough to have any significant Spherical characteristics. Think what it would mean. It would require a structure that had the heavy Bridging of a rigid Pyramid, yet somehow had the *absence* of Bridging needed for a free-flowing Sphere. It's just not possible. The rigidity would win, just like too much bureaucracy tends to stifle creativity."

The room sunk into gloomy silence as Harry poured coffee all around.

largely pure forms—the Pyramids, Cubes, Cylinders, and Spheres— with fuzzy boundaries between certain types. The levels of cooperation between different stability structures vary, as do the degree to which one structure can conform to another (Figure 9.3).

There's no problem in having fuzzy boundaries between the same type of stability structures. And although it's not ideal, fuzzy permeable boundaries may be acceptable between Pyramids and Cylinders because

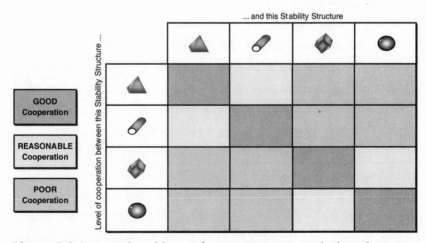

Figure 9.3 Potential problems of cooperating one with the other mean most stability structures should avoid overlapping.

TOM, DICK, AND HARRY—3

"What if we create *two* structures?" Tom suggested. "We could create a large Pyramid for the core training for the organization as a whole (with all the advantages of perceived continuity) and set up a Sphere to deal with the rapidly changing e-business component. If we get the two groups to interact closely, then we've solved the problem!"

It seemed like a potential solution until the group looked at Figure 9.3 and realized that getting a Pyramid and Sphere to cooperate closely would be extremely difficult. Not only were the perspectives entirely different, but so were the types of personalities. Back to the drawing board.

"Ah ha!" triumphed Harry, "I think I've got it! What if we combine both ideas: two *warped* structures. . . . As far as I can tell my existing training department is currently a pretty good Cylinder. What if we start from that foundation? Let's take most of the department and warp it a bit to give it more of a Pyramid feel. We can go for more incremental improvement of the training—each time we give a particular course, for example—rather than always wait for the annual review and overhaul. And we can try to keep a lot of the annual changes 'behind the scenes' so that people attending the training aren't even aware that things *have* changed. We'll freeze as much as possible the feedback forms, ways to register, training managers, locations, faculty, and so on, so that the Enablers and Triggers you guys keep going on about will hardly change.

"And then," he went on, "we can—this is the clever bit—create *another* warped version of the Cylinder that has more *Spherical* attributes! This is the one I'll set up to respond to the rapidly changing needs of the e-business group. But unlike when we talked about having a separate Pyramid and Sphere, *these* two structures *will* be able to cooperate well because they'll both share common parentage, so to speak. What do you think of that? I think I'm picking up all your jargon rather well, don't you think?"

"Yes and yes!" cried Tom.

"With a slight refinement . . . ," added Dick. He pointed to Figure 9.2. "Look at the relative ease of maintaining the different structures. The first you mentioned—the Cylinder-Pyramid—is *very* easy to maintain. Maybe the easiest of all the warped forms. Starting from your existing Cylinder and then adding the sort of Bridging you suggested (maintaining feedback forms, registration, and so on) and using Creep to replace Surge (going for additional small changes after each course rather than just overhauling once a year) should prove relatively easy. And it will indeed add many of the Pyramid characteristics Tom and I were hoping for to help keep the company glued together.

"But look at the structures again. Although there *is* a Cylinder-Sphere on the chart, it's shown as practically impossible to maintain. Think about it. Although the chart is based on observation over the years, it also makes intuitive sense. Although the pace of change in the Cylinder and Sphere are compatible, the Bridging in the Cylinder is still going to stifle the free flow of the Sphere—in the same way as we discussed earlier when we said the bureaucracy of a Pyramid would stifle creativity. So warping the Cylinder in the direction of a Sphere isn't practical. The Spherical components you try to add won't survive—at least not for long."

"Oh." Harry looked crestfallen.

"No, don't worry!" Dick quickly added, "I think your solution will still work. All we need to do is create a Sphere-Cylinder instead of a Cylinder-Sphere. I know that sounds like gibberish, but what I mean is let the *Sphere* characteristics dominate rather than those of the Cylinder. Look on the chart. Warping a Sphere to have more

Cylindrical attributes is almost as easy to maintain as the Cylinder-Pyramid we've already agreed on. Imagine that you set up a Sphere to handle the e-business group—just as you originally wanted to. But you don't let it be a full Sphere. Let me explain. You could run all sorts of unanticipated training "experiments" as needed, like a normal Sphere would. But you could ensure that *like a Cylinder*, once a year (when you conduct what remains of the overhaul for the rest of the business) you select which experiments in e-business training proved attractive for adoption by the rest of the company. These you build into the main training. So the "experiments" in the Sphere-Cylinder act as pilots—prototypes if you like—for your main training offerings in the Cylinder-Pyramid. The training program as a whole will remain at the cutting edge. The feeling of stability is maximized. And you, my friend, get to keep your job!"

"You know," smiled Harry, "I always rather liked the idea of being a warped personality. . . ."

they're dealing with the same sorts of known situations. Similarly, it's possible to have fuzzy boundaries between Cubes and Spheres because each is designed to deal with high levels of innovation. All other combinations should be avoided because the complexity of getting satisfactory cooperation among them is too much for management to sustain.

As we said at the beginning of this book, to thrive in a global economy, a swirl with a wide variety of innovation patterns, an organization needs a portfolio, perhaps with many examples of all four different stability structures. Some may exist in a slightly warped form. To manage that portfolio is no easy task, but guidelines are emerging:

- Deal with limited, higher-frequency turbulence by creating a subdomain, a stability structure in its own right. That is to say, to the degree that Spherical turbulence and Cylindrical turbulence come along, handle them separately.

- Recognize that managing this portfolio means leading groups of people with very different character traits. You want those different traits if the personnel are optimal for the structures they are within. While it's fine for the people within a given stability structure to share the same style, the organization's leadership needs to be able to identify with, communicate with, and cooperate with the different styles of each structure. This implies that the leadership group must be made up of individuals representing each of the four innovation styles. *This is probably the single greatest problem that we observe across companies,* for the leadership group is often made up of individuals sharing one or two dominant character traits. All four need to be represented.

- Consider organizing your company around similar types of stability structures. In modern, complex, global organizations, there easily can be many different ways to organize and it's easy to forget this essential point: The Enablers and Triggers, the management style, the time horizon, the level of planning, the form of reward system, the culture, the feedback mechanisms—all need to be focused on the appropriate form of stability structure above all else. Many policies, procedures, structures, and techniques are dependent on the different stability structures and vary greatly. So as companies use the appropriate stability structures in the different parts of their business, they need to recognize that the strategy, processes, resources, and organization of similar stability structures should have strong common denominators—and need to have stronger links to each other than they have to parts of the business organized into different forms of stability structures.

Our emphasis throughout this book is to help you maximize stable innovation rather than merely fixating on change. Sustained performance comes from creating a portfolio of stability structures that use different shock-absorbing techniques to minimize perceived disruption. In the next chapter we'll take a look at how one company has done just that.

CHAPTER 10

Energia

A case study in the power-generating industry

Energia, a fictitious electricity distribution company in the United States, was formed a decade ago through the merger of more than two dozen local companies. Its shares trade on the New York Stock Exchange. In 1999 Energia had revenues of roughly $17 billion. The company maintains more than 300 offices and has more than 25,000 employees.

A traditional engineering firm with a strong technical focus, the company is known worldwide for its technical supremacy. Most members of the top management are engineers. Historically, Energia has been bureaucratic, adapting gradually to changing conditions, occasionally going through a Lewin change. This was an adequate approach when change was infrequent.

Then the tidal wave hit, and Energia (which we have created as a composite of existing players in the field) could no longer adapt gradually. Many change programs only half succeeded. That is, they failed to achieve their goals, sometimes because the focus or objectives changed in midstream. Most change programs were over budget and late. Employees experienced an increasing number of wrenching changes. Other necessary changes could not be started because employees simply didn't have the time to do it all. Managers, too, were swamped with change programs that overrode normal business. Too many departments could no longer perform. Amid all this change and stress, the workload increased. Morale and motivation eroded. Change fatigue set in.

To find its way in this challenging environment, Energia has created an appropriate portfolio of stability structures. In the service development area, for example, Energia's main objective is to bring services to market in the shortest possible time. It does market analysis; it specifies, designs, and prepares the new services, then introduces them and supports them.

Competition among electricity distributors has radically changed the world of service development. It begins to show predominantly repetitive events (Figure 10.1). The dominant ones are the continuous introduction of services by the competition and the continuous increase of customer expectations. How Energia dealt with these challenges in a nondisruptive way is worth examining.

At first, service development was part of the product management and customer service departments. Each product manager was a separate profit center, deciding on and defining the improvement of the services. For customer service, which included after-sale service, output was measured in terms of customer satisfaction. Managers decided what upgrades were necessary and what investments were needed. After specifying their requirements, implementation was turned over to the operations department, but customer service remained responsible and coordinated the implementation itself.

One major problem was Enablers and Triggers of product management and customer service were geared to short-term successes related to revenue, margin, and customer satisfaction.

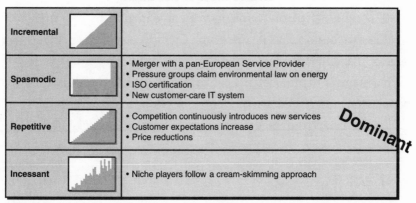

Selection of main events

Incremental		
Spasmodic		• Merger with a pan-European Service Provider • Pressure groups claim environmental law on energy • ISO certification • New customer-care IT system
Repetitive		• Competition continuously introduces new services • Customer expectations increase • Price reductions *Dominant*
Incessant		• Niche players follow a cream-skimming approach

Figure 10.1 For the service development area within the distribution company the world starts to show predominantly repetitive events.

For product management, the main Enabler for the people in those departments was the marketing director. The triggers the marketing director looked at were the revenue increase and the margin increase. The main Enabler for the customer service departments was the customer service director, who looked at the total cost and scores on performance indicators like ability, number of complaints, and operator friendliness.

But when drafted to perform service development activities, employees wound up with new Enabler and Trigger mechanisms, causing disruptions. The main Triggers for the product managers changed from a revenue-and-margin base to new product improvement. The changing Triggers lead to new Enablers, like the operations director who needs to give priority to, and agree with, those running development, as well as with the finance director who decides on the investments.

Customer service employees also found the Enabler and Trigger system changed when they added service department activities to their normal activities. The Triggers changed from the total costs to the improvement of a specific service level. Here, too, new Triggers brought new Enablers, namely, the IT development manager, who needs to give priority to these adjustments, as well as the product managers who need to support the initiative to get the required funding.

The result: Disruption for many people involved.

Energia found a solution. It set up a Cylinder structure for the service development. It built a service development cycle with employees specifically assigned to it, then set up Enabler and Trigger mechanisms for those people that buffered them from service development cycles.

Energia started by defining the cycle process (Figure 10.2):

1. Execute market analysis.

2. Specify new services.

3. Design and develop services.

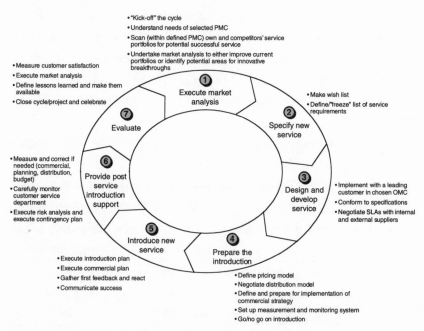

Figure 10.2 Build the service development cycles.

4. Prepare the introduction.

5. Introduce *new* services.

6. Provide postservice introduction support.

7. Evaluate.

At the end of each cycle, employees are back at the beginning because the evaluation can lead to new specifications of the service. The next step was to take this cyclical process and ensure that the Enabler and Trigger mechanisms for the employees were not affected by this planning.

Relying on shock-absorbing techniques, Energia introduced Bridging, setting up Triggers and Enablers that supersede service development cycles and remain constant for the people involved. These people are placed in a service development department, whose director holds them responsible only for service development innovations. This leads not only to stability for the people in service development but also for the people involved in these service developments from the line organization. That's because they have a clear, defined role and a standardized way of working with the service development people.

Energia also found a way to minimize the impact of the cycle's start. The Surging technique is used for this.

The Surge is facilitated in several ways, starting with standardized processes and roles that make it much easier for the people to get up to speed as part of the new team and with the new assignment. The availability and accessibility of knowledge needed—from both information and knowledge databases maintained by the company—is a big help. So, too, is the accessibility and availability of the people with the right knowledge to start these processes.

The Creeping and steering of service development cycles is done by a group of people who oversee product development, customer service management, and IT operations.

But Energia must deal with other turbulence as well. One major issue was its integration with a European alliance partner. Service development minimized the disruption from this integration by spreading it over several service introduction cycles. It regarded the integration as a series of service improvements. It identified the best practices for each process, based on key performance indicators in the two companies. It identified the best support tools in each company. It slowly brought the methods of operations of the two companies closer, by adding the implementation of a best practice or adding the switch to a new support tool to those already in service. When the methods of operations in the service development domain of each company was identical, then—and only then—could their integration be formalized.

So as Energia contemplates the continuing globalization and innovation of its core businesses, it feels confident that it has in place a portfolio of structures that maximize stability while allowing it to innovate frequently and remain a leader in the market. Energia should be able to grow smoothly in other markets because it can integrate acquisitions without causing operational problems. These skills should enable Energia to thrive in turbulent markets without frustrating its employees in the process.

Conceptually, we can now see how to sustain performance, to thrive and to escape the change dilemma—by creating a portfolio of structures that maximize stability with innovation built in, in the appropriate form. So how do you determine *what* forms of stable innovation you need? How do you find out *where* you need them? *How* do you actually make the changes? That's what we'll look at next.

CHAPTER 11

Drawing maps

Turning the corner
and focusing on innovation

We've seen how an organization in the global economy has to maximize four forms of stable innovation if it is to thrive amid turbulence without burning out. These stability structures can be built right into your organization, starting now. Let's tackle the nuts and bolts: How can we understand what turbulence is? How can we design stability? How do we change our company and its structures into an organization fit to cope with the challenges of turbulence? You have to

- Determine what turbulence is influencing or directly impacting your company. From that understanding create a turbulence map.

- Look over the map and decide how to organize your company using a portfolio of stability structures. Create an "innovation map" that will help you to design a path to stability.

How do you create a turbulence map that will track all the turbulence that hits your organization? You identify and analyze the most important strategic choices your company has made. You look at the current hot spots of change fatigue. You focus on the critical events in your industry. You analyze your company by each business domain and examine the turbulence relevant to that domain. From all this information, you create a turbulence map that enables you to see where to go (for most organizations, this analysis takes at least several weeks).

The first step in creating the map is to understand what turbulence is leading to change fatigue in your organization. This is a six-part process:

1. Understand the basic strategic choices for your company.

2. Identify hot spots of change fatigue. Everybody in the company knows of places where people have run out of energy because they've been subjected to too much change. Parts of the company may have had turnover rates of 20 percent or more. Identify *where* these hot spots are and *why* this is so.

3. Analyze the company and split it into its main business domains.

4. Identify, perhaps through a brain-storming session, the events happening throughout your company—the developments and trends inside and outside the company that you must deal with but that may *not* add to the change fatigue of your people.

5. Make a turbulence forecast for each domain. Identify all specific events in each domain. Then make an assessment: do these events collectively create turbulence within the domain?

6. Add the turbulence lists for each domain, creating a turbulence map of your organization.

Let's examine these steps in more detail.

Understand Strategic Choices. Start by asking yourself, "What is our mission? Why does our company exist? What value does it add for clients? What do we want to achieve? When?" At once simple and over-arching, these questions should provoke answers that will tell you what strategic constraints your company has set itself. Are there boundaries in scope, geography, or product service portfolio? Have you built boundaries based on values—deciding, for example, that you don't want to work in an industry that relies increasingly on genetic manip-ulation, or that you don't want to do business in countries where bribery is the norm? Examine your strategy of the last few years and try to understand what key decisions were made—and why. If possible, reduce everything to the fundamental question of what drives your strategy.

Identify Hot Spots of Change Fatigue. Interview your people, and try to understand where change fatigue exists and how it came about.

Is it a question of misfit? Or of overload? What drives resistance to change? Over the years we've found that people have many reasons for resisting change. Some people are just built that way; they resist any change. Many people just can't let go of the past. They see themselves as too old to change, or they don't want to. This frequently occurs in a postmerger environment but is a broader problem as well. In other cases, a company has reorganized too often or too quickly, and employees are unsettled. Or afraid of losing their jobs. Or people will say, "Our performance is extremely high; why should we change?" In a less general way, people can resist a particular change, or a certain project; they commonly bridle at the introduction of IT systems that require them to adapt to the machines, rather than vice versa. In some cases it's the learning curve involved, or their skepticism of the benefits to be derived, or the belief that this new system will too quickly become obsolete and be replaced itself.

In many cases, people don't know how to change. They don't get the leadership they need. They don't know where to go. They haven't figured out what their part of the change is. Often, peoples' resistance to change grows out of completely misaligned performance indicators after a series of reorganizations. If the last few years introduced a new appraisal system, many people are probably uncertain of how they are assessed and by whom. This is a complete misfit in Enabler and Trigger systems.

How widespread are these "people problems"? Ask around. Interviewing people about change reveals a good deal. Many times, we've found out through interviews that people say they're open to change but don't understand what's in it for them. Ask if they think the benefits realized from change programs match the investments made. Above all make clear that you really want to know what people think about changes.

Define the Business Domains. Carve the whole organization into domains, by which we mean sets of related activities sharing the same pattern of organization, that is, sharing similar Enabler and Trigger systems. Each should have one stability structure within it. Probably the easiest route is to view the business from the perspective of business processes. It may be that some parts of the business need to be separated into a domain of their own because the innovation pattern within them is very different and requires a different stability structure. You can recognize these clusters of activities within processes because they share equivalent Enabler and Trigger systems. You should wind up with 10 to 15 domains per company.

Identify Events. Start by taking stock of the scenario work that has been done in your company, including market forecasts and competitive analysis, to determine potential uncertainties. Examine the risk analyses that have been done in scenario workshops. Try to determine whether your company has a biased view on its own performance, whether it has blind spots. Look for any pattern of disasters that has befallen your company. Perhaps you'll find developments that you didn't want to see or were unable to see, now illuminated by hindsight. Look at other companies and other industries to see how they are reacting and what they are reacting to; no doubt you'll find some industries that appear to be farther along the road than you are. Some events of recent times have been Y2K, the introduction of the euro, the waves of national elections, the waves of mergers, and the noticeable shift in demography, including the aging of the world population. Such generic events can cause turbulence in some of your business domains.

Make a Turbulence Forecast for Each Domain. Step by step, select the events relevant to each domain. Then identify which cycles and events are specific to any one domain, such as the marketing cycle in your marketing department, the end-of-year cycle in the finance department, or the 18-month development and engineering cycle in the production department. Now use the Hibernation test (discussed in Chapter 5) to determine whether these events are potentially turbulent. Try to use the Hibernation test for each specific event, as well as for the whole set of events. Remember, as we said earlier, that not all disruptions are equal: some potential outcomes of the Hibernation test will be below the disruption level of people within a domain and so will not create turbulence. Finally, make a list of the key turbulence for each domain.

Create a Turbulence Map of Your Organization. The list of key turbulences by domain indicates where you are vulnerable to change fatigue. Then, through analysis, determine what turbulence you are able to influence or eliminate. Some potential turbulence can be neutralized, either by reducing the chance of occurrence, by eliminating the cause of the turbulence, or by shifting the point of impact to some other party.

In some cases, the impact of turbulence can be reduced by fragmenting one big bang into smaller bursts whose impact is more manageable. You might also renegotiate with parties involved in the turbulence, reducing its impact. Contingency planning might help reduce the impact, or at least help to better absorb it.

You might be able to solve whatever problem is causing the turbulence. If the turbulence stems from a competitor, for example, would acquisition of it solve the problem? If the turbulence stems from a political problem, can effective lobbying make it subside? Or you might relocate your activities, withdrawing from turbulent areas. Another desirable solution is to shunt the turbulence to some other party. Outsourcing can be an effective strategy here. If your company's call center for complaint handling is a source of turbulence, could you outsource complaint handling? If IT is causing turbulence, as it does in so many organizations, outsourcing might shunt the turbulence to your supplier. Some companies even outsource R&D to eliminate turbulence. Or they acquire innovative new companies that have experience dealing with a specific turbulence.

These options explored, you are ready to place the domains on the turbulence map (Figure 11.1).

The map's horizontal axis represents the frequency of turbulence. The vertical axis represents the level of innovation required to handle the

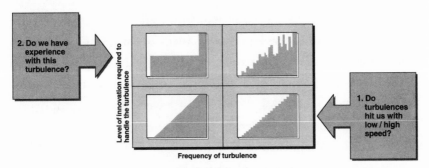

Figure 11.1 Draw the turbulence map.

turbulence. Do you have experience handling it? Or is this kind of turbulence completely new to you, so you must develop a way to handle it?

Plotting the domains on the map is a two-step exercise. First, decide in which of the four quadrants the domain would be placed. This is relatively simple because you know whether you have experienced the problem and whether the turbulence is a constant stream or an infrequent occurrence. So the upper-left quadrant would contain the domains where you have not experienced the turbulence, and you know that frequency is relatively low. In the lower-left quadrant you put the turbulence that you have handled before and where the frequency is low. The lower-right quadrant is for domains where you have experienced the turbulence and where frequency is higher. And the upper-right quadrant holds those domains where you have not experienced the turbulence and where frequency is high.

The second step in this process is to try to calibrate the domains within each quadrant. In effect, each quadrant becomes a "minigrid," and you assess the domains one by one and place them accordingly.

During this "pin the tail on the donkey" exercise in plotting the domains on the grid, you will find yourself defining and redefining the different domains. You will start with your current business processes as the leading business domains. But as you discuss frequency of turbulence and whether you have the experience to cope with a specific turbulence, you will find that certain processes are better split up and others better combined. You will find that certain Enabler-and-Trigger systems within processes belong together. So you'll find yourself going back and redefining some domains.

Finally you take stock of what you have. This is an important moment—the moment of transition from worrying about turbulence to planning for stability. You know the turbulence, and where and how hard it will hit you. You have identified how the turbulence influences people's Enabler-and-Trigger systems. With all this information, you can now plan for action to end the turbulence, by creating stability in the different domains of the organization. For this, you'll need an innovation map (Figure 11.2), which points out which structures need to be built for each domain. Stay focused on creating stability and implementing stable innovation.

This innovation map grows out of the turbulence map. The horizontal axis again represents frequency of innovation, the vertical axis

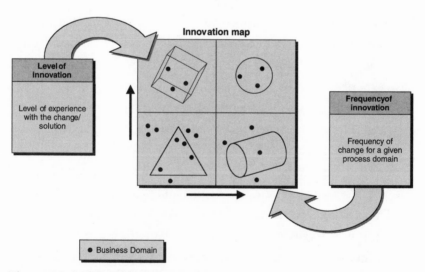

Figure 11.2 Draw the innovation map.

the degree of innovation and the degree of experience available. Now, along with the specific domains plotted within the grid, we have superimposed the stability structures—Pyramid, Cylinder, Cube, and Sphere—in their respective environments. These structures will provide the basis for talking about solutions and planning action, which is the focus of Part 2 and Part 3 of this book. First, however, we'll take a close look at how one company has used these mapping techniques.

CHAPTER 12

Coco

How a communication services company used an innovation map

et's examine how the innovation map worked for Coco, a communications services company that offers public relations, advertising, and strategic communications services to major clients around the world. Established in 1976, Coco (a composite of several companies in the field) has its head office in Europe and has 16 offices worldwide. It is owned by 10 senior executives, three of whom founded the company. Well regarded, Coco is able to attract the people it wants. The company distinguishes itself through its creation of original products and services.

Through a series of workshops, Coco's management learned how to organize its business (Figure 12.1).

It identified 15 business domains and plotted them in the matrix. In the *Cube* area (upper left), Coco decided to put its product development domain and its key account acquisition domain. In the *Pyramid* (lower

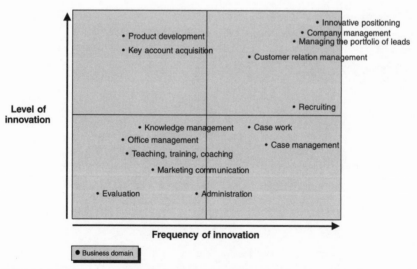

Figure 12.1 Coco went through an end-of-change trajectory to understand how it could organize its business.

left) quadrant, it placed its human resources assessment domain because management agreed that it *did not* want to change frequently the way it evaluated and assessed its people. In the same quadrant are knowledge management, office management, marketing communication, teaching, training, coaching, and administration. Going through the process, management realized that while the company had been established 23 years ago with an entrepreneurial approach, it was now time for certain areas of activities to be organized hierarchically. This understanding was a breakthrough for management, especially the three founders.

In the *Cylinder* quadrant (lower right), Coco plotted assignment execution and assignment management. Many consulting companies and other professional services firms organize themselves similarly. As an innovative company that delivers creative services systems itself, Coco put certain domains in the *Sphere* quadrant. Client management should offer innovatively what is needed for their client rather than promoting from the shelf. This placement helped them to recruit entrepreneurial people in the field of communications, rather than production-oriented marketing experts. Innovative positioning, company management, and managing the portfolio of potential assignments were also classified as Spheres.

During the pin-the-tail-on-the-donkey exercise, Coco's management wound up spending considerable time uncovering and codifying the different domains. Trying to understand the degree of innovation necessary and whether each domain had the ability to cope with innovation, management learned it did not have a shared vision. The exercise made clear that arriving at such an understanding takes time and requires at least a few cycles of pinning the tail on the donkey to develop a shared understanding of what the company's experience meant.

By looking at four examples where Coco applied stability structures to domains, we will see how the company created an environment in which people could handle turbulence without disruption and change fatigue: a Pyramidal structure for knowledge management; a Cylinder for execution of assignments; a Cube for the product development group, which designs and develops services; and a Sphere for client management.

Knowledge Management. Coco's management decided to centralize knowledge management and decentralize knowledge application. Knowledge management is responsible for uncovering, storing, maintaining, and enriching data and information. It uses modern techniques such as intelligent agents and browsing techniques to make information accessible throughout the firm. Knowledge application, however, is driven so much by other domains in the company that it made sense to decentralize it to the different domains.

The external events that impact Coco's knowledge management seem ripe with potential turbulence. Internal questions constantly arise within knowledge management. Many people working in knowledge management were busy with understanding what the Y2K problem would mean to them and whether their systems would be ready for it. Because knowledge management is built on IT, many people felt the pressure of learning to adapt to new systems. A constant stream of information within and outside the company added to the burden of knowledge management.

Apply the Hibernation test to the people within knowledge management and it becomes clear that despite all these responsibilities, only a few areas of potential turbulence loom. Y2K was definitely one of them. Putting in new IT systems was also potentially disruptive. Potential highly frequent disruptive events like client questions and the constantly changing information stream turn out not to be disruptive because Coco decided to organize knowledge management in such a way that people within knowledge management were not responsible for the applications of the knowledge. This responsibility always resides with the client.

How was knowledge management organized? Around a central core staff responsible for data gathering, storing, maintaining, and enriching. For the major industry groups, a client knowledge manager was responsible for maintaining relationships with individual client teams. The knowledge management group discovered long ago that the way to interact with the client teams is to anticipate possible information needs rather than wait and see. Success is defined by how successfully support is rendered in the long term, not by the response to individual questions. Typically, 99 percent of knowledge management's work can be anticipated; overtime is rare. Having in place the latest technology and system support are keys to staying on top of the problems. Knowledge management's most popular product is its early morning hints briefing.

Assignment Execution. Coco's assignments typically last weeks to months and are mostly focused on helping clients design and launch advertising campaigns. Coco also helps clients develop branding and positioning strategies because it discovered years ago that the earlier it was involved in market positioning, the better it could perform later. About 80 percent of Coco's continuing assignments originate from the existing customer base; 70 percent of that amount originates from its 40 largest customers worldwide. For those largest customers, Coco also provides specialized public relations advice and management communications training and counseling. Assignments are typically run from the office where the account director of Coco's clients is situated.

To carry out a typical assignment, the assignment director establishes an assignment team, consisting of members of the account team and individual creative consultants. The team most often is completed by adding support staff and, if needed, specialists from such areas as market research or public relations. Responsibility for running the assignment is in the hands of the account director, while day-to-day management is mostly in the hands of an account team member. The creative consulting department within an office is officially managed by the office manager; unofficially, the consultants themselves are responsible for being profitable.

A look at the external events that impact Coco's assignment execution shows a portfolio of possible turbulence. First, of course, is the content and the context of the assignment on hand. What is the subject? What timing is needed? What is the issue? What are the capabilities necessary for success? Which individuals are involved? What is the role of each individual? How is the leadership constituted? What is the leadership style? How is client interaction assignment established and managed? Almost every aspect of an assignment could be disrupting for the individuals on the assignment team.

Remember the main responsibility in handling an assignment is to satisfy the customer, meeting expectations and attempting to exceed them. By definition, that's very subjective. For all the individuals working on an assignment, all aspects of this are potentially disruptive and put enormous pressure on the organization and especially on the assignments in Coco.

How does Coco deal with this? Day-to-day responsibility for managing the funnel of new assignments and thereby managing the potential assignments rests with individual client-team leaders and the office manager. They manage the assignment stream and decide on assignment leadership. Individual assignment leaders recruit internally for their assignment teams, making their needs known in the internal "marketplace" and seeing who is available, though of course management must make the final assignments. Team leaders are measured not just by client satisfaction but by team satisfaction. In the long term, then, team leaders need to care for individual team members in order to succeed. Team members are measured most importantly on their individual contribution to the team and also on the team's success overall. Biannually every individual is assessed on performance, based on multiple assignment assessments done by the office's core partners and the industry group. By performing this Bridging technique, Coco ensures that individuals are assessed primarily on long-term development performance and multiple assignments rather than on an individual role on one assignment.

Product Development. Responsible for designing and developing services for the whole company, this domain has undergone major changes. Two years ago Coco's management realized that the Internet was affecting both how it did business with clients and how clients did business generally. It also accepted that this was likely to accelerate. A companywide working group was established to take stock and suggest how to proceed. Because of the press of daily business, the working group took a full year to report its conclusion: throughout the company various initiatives were under development that were leading to unfocused resources and deployment, inconsistent communication with clients, and, above all, the lack of a consistent services philosophy.

Six months later, a leader was recruited for the newly established strategic services group, with the responsibility of leading a companywide new media initiative. The core of his plan was to focus service development for 3 to 5 years on how the Internet and related developments would affect Coco's customers. A key part of this new leader's plan was to organize people into industry groups, which on the one hand would increase Coco's knowledge of the industry by working with customers worldwide, while on the other hand it could support the new service package rollout through these same industry groups. Within the industry groups the strategic services group identified two or three leading clients with whom Coco agreed to invest in a joint 3-year program to understand how the Internet could affect clients and to develop Internet-related packages for branding and positioning, advertisement, and public relations.

This joint investment created a 30-person Internet knowledge center within strategic services, with offices in Palo Alto, California; New York, and Sofia Antipolis, France, whose only objective is to stay abreast of what's going on the Web. All companywide investments in brochures and presentations of what Coco could do for clients on Internet issues has halted. All Coco's activities concerning Internet-related new developments for clients are now concentrated in this group. Two core industry groups, finance and telecoms, are in the process of launching new media campaigns. The strategic services group developed a package called "Finternet" for a financial institution in the United States. It also led a European telecommunications company through the creative process to come up with a "mobility meets the Internet" product, a way of using prepaid calling cards to access the Internet. The strategic services group then created an attractive advertisement and promotion campaign.

The product development group's environment shows possible turbulence. The key turbulence comes from wishes of new key clients, the changes in their industries, and the technology trends that might affect them. All these might well influence the environment for people in the product development group. How is the group organized? The head of this group chairs its meetings, while decisions are made by a steering committee that consists of the leading client account managers of Coco's largest clients. They ultimately decide on what service is to be developed and with which clients it might be developed. They're also responsible for carrying out a replication plan within Coco.

The product development domain is very much a project organization, with several service development projects running in parallel. The individuals in the group are supervised and assessed only by the head of the group. Their success depends on two things: client feedback and whether a solution can be replicated. The development effort in a project is always managed by someone from the product development group with only one direct client: the client manager for the leading customer. The combined replication effort is managed by the same team, and the head of the group is the ultimate client.

Client Management. Using Spherical principles, Coco has organized its responsibility for handling client relationships within account teams led by an account director, rather than a "one-person sales force." This allows Coco to better play the numbers game. Coco's account director generally has contacts on the highest level within the client organization. Assignments, typically, originate from several directions. In some cases, clients bring problems to Coco or refer new clients. In other cases, Coco actively seeks assignments by proclaiming how it can solve specific problems for its clients.

The accounts teams' objectives are to maximize Coco's business within the client by maximizing the clients' value. It wants to create a balance in the level of assignments carried out, with assignments on a strategic level but also a stream of assignments on the operational level. Coco wants a balanced stream of assignments to smooth deployment of its people, and it only wants to win jobs where it can distinguish itself. Coco does not want jobs where it knows other companies can do superior work.

Client management's environment shows potential turbulence. Key positions in the client organization could shift: people could leave or be dismissed or be switched unexpectedly into new jobs. Indeed, such changes happen almost weekly. Clients can produce unexpected behavior, including unanticipated questions. The competitive position of the client might change dramatically, either in areas where Coco is strong, creating opportunities, or where Coco is not strong, creating challenges. Because the account director's main responsibility is to manage relations with the client and to maximize the value to Coco, the director must manage the funnel of potential assignments constantly. All these events are potentially turbulent for the account team if Coco does not enable the team to play the numbers game.

Coco's horizon for planning is generally 3 to 6 months. The account team tries to serve the client optimally with weekly planning to balance the stream of potential assignments, with weekly meetings to report on the status of assignments, and with quarterly meetings to update the tactical and strategic choices made on the client's behalf. There's also a yearly meeting to ensure that the learning continues within the client team. The account team plays the numbers game to ensure a balanced business stream: to understand the potential value of a potential assignment, to understand the potential success and the chance of success, but also to understand the timing of the deliverables.

Having studied Coco, we are ready to move on. We have investigated the hot spots of change fatigue. Much as Coco's management did, managers can work out, by consulting the innovation map, where their company should be. They can determine where they want to be, what the potential problems are, and how to bridge the gap. This involves three steps:

1. Align the stabilizing factors.
2. Align the Motivator, Enabler, and Trigger systems of people in the domains.
3. Start applying the mental model created in day-to-day business decisions.

In Part 2, we'll introduce the art and practice of stabilization.

AIDE MÉMOIRE

1. In a rapidly changing global business environment, companies must learn to deal with different patterns of innovation:
   - *Incremental innovation,* appropriate for environments that are only occasionally disrupted, and then by factors that the organization knows how to deal with.
   - *Spasmodic innovation,* needed when organizations only occasionally have to deal with one-time change, and there's a big pulse that goes through the organization as it shifts from one form to another.
   - *Repetitive innovation,* best for organizations that face frequent change of a recurring nature, one after another after another.
   - *Incessant innovation,* for organizations that face fast and furious changes they've never experienced before, with challenges coming from all directions.

Innovation Map

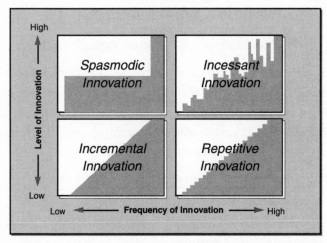

Stability structures: for each pattern of innovation there is a practical structure that optimizes performance by maximizing disruption.

2. Each of the four needs its own practical structure to optimize performance and minimize disruption.

Pyramids maintain stability in an environment of incremental innovation, following a strategy of slow adaptation and occasional avoidance. The key words are *perfection* and *continuity.* The mental model of the Pyramid individual is

Professionalism = steady progression + no surprises

Cubes maximize periods of stability by clustering spasmodic innovation into short, efficient bursts. The key words are *preparation* and *timing.* The mental model of the Cube individual is

Professionalism = effective transition + efficient consolidation

Cylinders minimize disruption by building repetitive innovation into their processes. The key words are *efficiency* and *learning.* The mental model of the Cylinder individual is

Professionalism = expertise + new challenges

Spheres reduce disruption amid incessant innovation by developing the maximum number of options, then selecting the most stable. The key words are *assessment* and *action.* The mental model of the Sphere individual is

Professionalism = flexibility + opportunism

3. All the structures provide stability and foster innovation amid turbulence. Remember that turbulence is disruptive to people *only when it is perceived as a significant culture change* for the organization. That is, it affects "how things really work around here"—the unwritten rules of an organization.

Three main drivers determine an organization's culture:

- *Motivators:* what is important to you.
- *Enablers:* who is important to you because they can grant or withhold that Motivator.
- *Triggers:* what the Enabler will look at to decide whether you get what is important to you.

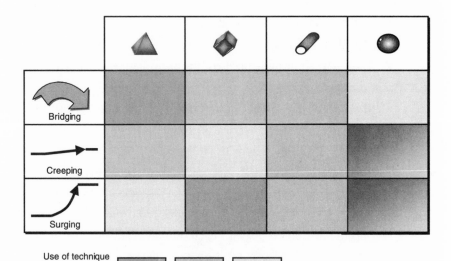

Each stability structure applies the techniques according to consistent principles.

But disruption to these drivers can be minimized through these "shock absorbers."

- *Bridging,* which provides continuity by maintaining select Enablers and Triggers that span potentially disruptive events. *Bridge* as much as possible.

- *Creeping* absorbs minor potential turbulence into a gradual drift of rigorously aligned Enablers and Triggers. *Creep* as needed unless the end goal is too far off to be reached in time.

- *Surging* smoothes major potential turbulence by accelerating aligned shifts of Enablers and Triggers to the maximum nondisruptive levels. *Surge* when Creep is not sufficient.

4. Because no company can rely on just one stability structure to deal with turbulence, it must develop a portfolio of structures in a two-part process: Determine what turbulence is influencing or directly affecting your company and create a *turbulence map.* Then look over the map and decide how to organize your company using a portfolio of stability structures, and create an innovation map.

To create a turbulence map:

- Understand your basic strategic choices.
- Identify hot spots of change fatigue.
- Analyze the company and split it into its main business domains.
- Identify developments and trends inside and outside the company that you must deal with but which may or may *not* add to the change fatigue of your people.
- Make a turbulence forecast for each domain. Identify all specific events in each domain. Then make an assessment: do these events collectively create turbulence within the domain?
- Add the turbulence lists for each domain, creating a turbulence map of your organization.

The *innovation map* grows out of the turbulence map. Superimpose the stability structures—Pyramid, Cylinder, Cube, and Sphere—in their respective environments. These structures will provide the basis for talking about solutions and planning action.

Part 2

Strategy, Tactics, and Operations

CHAPTER 13

Learning about stabilizers

Six aspects of an organization that bolster stability

L et's take stock of where we are. If you had applied to your own company each of the concepts covered in Part 1 of this book, you would by now know which stability structures you wanted in which parts of your organization. To achieve this, you would have first analyzed your firm's business environment to gain some understanding of the patterns of turbulence affecting different parts of the company. Then you would have hypothesized where the boundaries of those business domains were—by looking at sets of related activities—and refined those boundaries into subdomains that shared the same pattern of turbulence. Finally, based on the dominant pattern within each domain, you would have decided on the appropriate stability structure for each domain, and thought about the corresponding combinations of Bridging, Creeping, and Surging techniques needed to minimize perceived disruption.

Now it would be time to reinforce the stability structures you were trying to achieve. How?

A new mindset—striving for stable innovation—needs to drive all those responsible for implementing the appropriate Bridging, Creeping, and Surging, especially those people within each domain who make detailed design decisions and operational decisions. All these peoples' decisions must be aimed at maximizing stability, by using the appropriate stability structures, in order to minimize perceived disruption and so avoid change fatigue.

No *small* group of individuals, however brilliant, can make all the decisions needed to reap the benefits of an aligned portfolio of stability structures. Not only is the detail of the design too complex to think of centrally, but the trade-offs and repercussions of decisions are themselves too interconnected and complex for any individual or small group to work out. A whole organization, however, can *collec-*

tively make the right aligned decisions—provided everyone shares the same mindset.

It would be simplistic, however, to suggest that merely disseminating a shared mental model of stable innovation throughout an organization is sufficient to maximize perceived stability. In reality, people do not have the time or energy to go back to first principles on every decision they make. So, to be practical, we must *also* draw on the broad foundation of knowledge that already exists about how the concept of stable innovation translates into key processes of a business. In other words, instead of returning to first principles, we need to apply the lessons learned by others.

Based on our experience with clients, we have determined that six related facets of any organization—Strategy, Tactics, Operations, Teamwork, Quality, and Communication—are fundamental to stable innovation, irrespective of which stability structures are employed.

Three of these facets focus on content, that is, doing the *right things to maximize stability:*

- Strategy
- Tactics
- Operations

Three focus on process, that is, doing things in the right ways to maximize stability:

- Teamwork
- Quality
- Communication

In trying to see the implications of applying the mental model of stable innovation to these six facets, we focused on those components that have the greatest potential for maximizing stability—in other words those components that are catalysts for stability. An organization that builds up these particular components of Strategy, Tactics, Operations, Teamwork, Quality, and Communication is likely to enhance its stability significantly (in addition to whatever gains are realized from applying the shock-absorbing techniques—Bridging, Creeping, and Surging—already discussed).

The greatest stabilizing component of *Strategy* is the ability to identify potential turbulence by looking beyond people's current mental models. *Tactics* can ensure that the strategic choices are followed and translated into understandable language for operations, resulting in the most stable passage. *Operations* can ensure that routes that maximize stability are followed. The aspect of *Teamwork* that provides a great leverage point for maximizing stability are followed. The aspect of *Teamwork* that provides a great leverage point for maximizing stability is to create an environment in which individuals can excel. For *Quality* it's a question of creating safe environments where groups progressively learn to innovate. For *Communication* it's tuning communications to the specific requirements of different stability structures so as to align behavior across the whole organization.

Leveraging these six facets of a business are not the only possible choices for maximizing stability, but interwoven they address all the key aspects of organizational content and process (Figure 13.1). Each can help minimize disruption in all four stability structures, although it must be applied differently in each.

In a Pyramid, for example, Communication reinforces the consistency of the structure while measuring and encouraging aligned incremental improvement. It also helps prevent any transition through Creep from breaking up into a Lewin change. In a Cube, Communication enhances stability by stressing continuity despite the transitions, as well as encourages rapid aligned behavior during the transitions. In a Cylinder, Communication enhances stability by increasing the smoothness within cycles and the transition between cycles by providing access to appropriate know-how and reinforcing

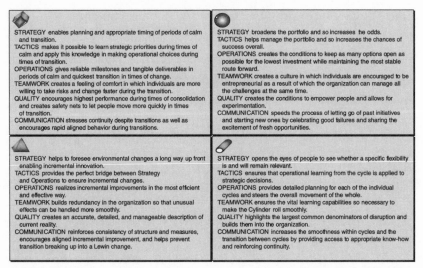

Figure 13.1 How stabilizers contribute to creating stability in the different stability structures.

continuity that further enhances the smoothness. In a Sphere, Communication enhances stability by speeding the process of letting go of past initiatives and of starting new ones through celebrating good failures and sharing the excitement of fresh opportunities.

As we'll see in coming pages, these six aspects do indeed enhance stability when applied appropriately. From structure to structure, how each should be applied varies, sometimes subtly, sometimes radically. As we examine in detail how each Stabilizer needs to be applied to each structure, we'll also show how applying the Stabilizers in ways that are inappropriate—or not applying them at all—increases the chance of disruption and can even create disruption.

We will now look through our chosen six facets of a business at the details of how to apply the mindset of stable innovation. For the Strategy Stabilizer we will look at breaking through barriers of thought. For the Tactics Stabilizer we'll explore connecting thinking and doing. In the Operations Stabilizer we will show how to focus on the destination. Then we'll consider the Teamwork Stabilizer and how to look at collaborative stability through individualism. With the Quality Stabilizer we'll discuss how to ensure performance by allowing mistakes. And with the Communication Stabilizer we'll learn about applying the power of the word. We'll start, in the next chapter, with Strategy.

CHAPTER 14

Breaking through the thought barrier

Learning to look beyond current mental models

U nderstanding your thought barriers offers enormous untapped potential for strengthening strategy to support stable innovation.

Existing mental models can act as thought barriers that prevent an organization from identifying and foreseeing turbulence, which in turn can lead to disruptive change. Becoming wedded to a particular mental model can prevent organizations from identifying unknown, unexpected, or unwanted events that need to be taken into account as strategy is formulated. In some cases, the consequences of events are unwanted, and so the events are simply ignored. In other cases, unexpected events are ignored because the mental model of the organization simply does not account for them. The consequences that these unidentified events can have on an organization are considerable and often lead directly to disruption. Thought barriers must be overcome to identify all possible events and to create or maintain stability within each stability structure. To achieve this, you must make explicit the consequences of these currently unidentified events and account for them in your strategies to maintain stability.

How can existing thought barriers be overcome? We'll start by looking at the tools available to go beyond your mental model—in other words, to identify and understand the turbulence, uncertainties, and environmental changes. Then we'll look at how to combine the tools to foresee turbulence within each stability structure.

In the Pyramid, we will show how these tools and this strategy help to foresee environmental changes far in advance, enabling incremental innovation. For the Cube, we will show how these tools and this strategy help identify plans and prepare people for the periods of calm and transition. For the Cylinder, we will show how this approach opens peoples' eyes, so they can see what specific flexibility is relevant by identifying trends and changes. For the Sphere, these tools will broaden the portfolio of opportunities and identify the best ones, thus increasing the odds of success.

A variety of tools are available to look beyond your current mental model from different perspectives:

- A *nightmare competitor* helps to identify your internal weaknesses, by imagining the worst possible competitor and seeing how it attacks your organization.

- *Role playing* shows various outcomes that would result from different philosophies of interacting with your competitors, suppliers, and customers.

- *Game playing* helps you understand the assumptions you make about the rules of the market. This can provide understanding of which rules are explicit, which are unwritten, and which can be broken or bent.

- *Pattern recognition* helps you understand the trends you are following and allows for learning from other industries that are a step ahead.

- *Scenario planning* gives you insight into the uncertainties of the market, helping you prepare robust strategies for whatever might unfold.

We'll look at each, in turn, in the next few chapters.

CHAPTER 15

Sweet dreams

Imagine your "worst nightmare,"

then learn how to overcome it

The "nightmare competitor" tool, its name notwithstanding, will help you sleep at night. You imagine a strategy that could slaughter you, carried out by a competitor that employs all its strong competencies. The competitor is unrestrained by the operational barriers that exist within your organization. In a nightmare competitor workshop you go through a thought process:

1. Envision a realistic consortium that contains all the competencies needed to be the best-in-class player in the market.

2. Join this consortium (at least in your mind), and bring with you a strategic goal of slaughtering your previous employer.

3. Identify the strategies your new company will need to achieve its goal.

4. Rejoin your original company and create an action plan that transforms *it* into a nightmare competitor.

5. Keep the mirror that illuminates your weaknesses on the wall of the boardroom. That way, at every decision, you will be reminded to anticipate what your nightmare competitor would do.

Let's turn to the telecommunications industry to see how this method might play out.

1. The consortium you assemble requires world-class network design, rights of way, world-class customer care, marketing competencies, and service development expertise, as well as unlimited funding, lobbying power, and some "content" that provides you a competitive advantage. Having identified the desired competencies, go to other industries to see who has them.

1. You assemble a list and from that identify the consortium partners that provide these "best-in-class" competencies (Figure 15.1). The new company is called Miracles and pulls together the competencies of MCI Worldcom, IBM, various railways, Airtouch, Citigroup, Lufthansa, Eurocard, and Sony.

2. Form a strong management team for Miracles (all participants in the exercise take up seats on the management team). Your employer may have fired you, but your experience and competencies make you attractive to Miracles; create a résumé that reflects this background.

At the first meeting of Miracles' management team, each other player is given a false identity and a résumé as an employee of one of the consortium partners (Figure 15.2). You each take on this role of a successful and aggressive manager. Management's mission with this new consortium is to capture more than 50 percent of your old company's customers. This is, of course, very ambitious.

3. During the first board meeting, decide on the strategic thrusts that will take you to your goal.

These might include:

- Use the networks of the shareholders (railway, cable company, mobile operator) to build a strong presence quickly.

- Start selling to large customers quickly, using account managers from your shareholders, because they already have significant relationships with these customers.

- Bring your lobbying power to bear, where appropriate, to speed up approvals and waivers involving regulations, licenses, and so on.

- Keep your competitor busy by hiring several large law firms in this market and letting them find ways to make trouble for your previous employer. They might, for example, fire a salvo

Contributed Competence	Potential Consortium Partner
Infrastructure	AT&T, MCI Worldcom, SITA
Rights of way	Railways, Utilities, Cable
Marketing	Sony, EDS, Microsoft
Customer Care	Airlines, Credit card companies
Installing and maintaining services	Rank Xerox, EDS
Money/power	Citicorp, Shell
Content	McGraw-Hill

Consortium Partner	Key Strengths Contributed
• MCI Worldcom	• World-class network design • World-class operations experience • Customer knowledge • International coverage of service and customer care
• IBM	• Possibility of providing integrated services • Outstanding business services and project management
• Rail	• Right of way • Infrastructure (overlay) • Lobby power
• Airtouch/Vodafone	• World-class mobile infrastructure • Global mobile consumer and business reach
• Citicorp	• Unlimited funding • Lobby power
• Lufthansa	• Excellent customer care, loyalty • International customer-care coverage
• Eurocard	• Consumer distribution outlets • Excellent customer care • International customer-care coverage
• Sony	• World-class consumer marketing

Figure 15.1 Example Telecom: Service provider Miracles. Assemble a realistic consortium that contains all the competencies to be the "best in class" player in your market.

You are Jim "Rambo" Smith, a member of the board of Miracles

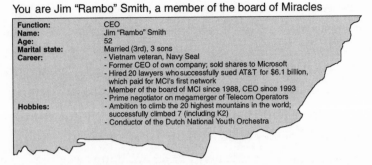

Function:	CEO
Name:	Jim "Rambo" Smith
Age:	52
Marital state:	Married (3rd), 3 sons
Career:	- Vietnam veteran, Navy Seal
	- Former CEO of own company; sold shares to Microsoft
	- Hired 20 lawyers who successfully sued AT&T for $6.1 billion, which paid for MCI's first network
	- Member of the board of MCI since 1988, CEO since 1993
	- Prime negotiator on megamerger of Telecom Operators
Hobbies:	- Ambition to climb the 20 highest mountains in the world; successfully climbed 7 (including K2)
	- Conductor of the Dutch National Youth Orchestra

Figure 15.2 You are Jim "Rambo" Smith, a member of the board of Miracles. "Leave" your old company and join the consortium.

of complaints to regulatory authorities about various aspects of your competitor's operations.

· Lure and keep the best people employed by your original employer.

4. Now revert to your real job ("Fired? That must have been a misunderstanding."). You first ask if somehow you can stop the formation of the nightmare competitor. A legitimate question and a most effective counter if it is possible, but in all cases we have seen this has not been the case. So let us say, "No. This nightmare competitor will challenge us." You then must consider: Can we become the nightmare competitor ourselves? What stops us from all the strategic thrusts it would use? You will find, after root-cause analysis, that the answer is "Nothing." So you consider:

· What competencies and processes are needed?

· What weaknesses must we address and what strengths can we build on?

· What needs to be urgently changed to prepare us for new competition?

In our telecom example, management learned that its mental model kept it from recognizing that product introductions were too slow and that customers demanded better service. By exercising through the competencies of a best-in-class competitor, assembled from all industries, managers were able to look beyond their mental model about the possible speed of product introductions and the service levels offered to customers. After all, if others set higher standards, why couldn't they? This helped them understand that internal inefficiencies were a potential threat, and that they could improve if they wanted to.

Preparing early for this new phase, by taking away the internal inefficiencies and designing and implementing a fast service creation process, the telecom company prepared for a new phase with minimum disruption. It avoided changing priorities frequently, which causes major internal disruptions. This had happened frequently in the past and had become a breakpoint when facing new competition. The nightmare competitor exercise also helped avoid disruptions in the development of products and services. Internal process inefficiencies were identified and removed, and the process was modified to meet higher customer service demand.

The lessons learned should continue to influence your daily decision making. So keep that mirror that illuminates your weaknesses on the wall. Always bear in mind and try to anticipate what that nightmare competitor would do.

The play's the thing

Role playing aligns the actions and the energy of people with those of the company

The *role-playing* tool helps you understand possible roles that you could play in the industry, as well as roles your competitors might play. In scenario thinking you try to define a role within different futures. Role playing turns this inside out. Instead of different future environments, you explore different roles or ambitions within a vision of the future. Role playing aligns the actions and the energy of your people and your company and the mental model of them that needs to be focused on achieving this role.

How do you get started with role playing? Forecast a world as it might evolve, breaking loose from what is currently possible. Then envision the future of your industry. Within this future, envision the different roles an industry player might have (Figure 16.1). Finally, analyze the impact of performing the role yourself and also of a competitor taking the role. See how these different approaches work out, relative to each other. After you have seen the relative success of the possible roles, select the role you like best and plan strategic thrusts to realize this ambition.

Let's see how this might play out in the transport industry. The first step is to take the people out of the existing environment to a future far enough away to allow for creativity. This future must have some relevance to your expected planning, so envision your industry in terms of the strategic dimensions that best capture how it is structured. What does the value chain look like? What are customer demands? What do products look like? How are they delivered? Who competes?

With these roles identified, plot how each will play in the future, relating them to the different dimensions you have envisioned (Figure 16.2). Analyze the impact the role can have, both internally (what value do you need to create, what competencies are needed, what profit margins are sustainable) and externally (clients, suppliers, competitors).

Roles	Description
Rule breaker	New rail operators break with the rules of traditional monopolistic railway companies. They are customer oriented, develop competitive services, develop one-stop shopping services, etc.
Game player	Manufacturers and logistic service providers have become game players. They provide and share information on their logistics and transport requirements by which it is possible to optimize logistics and transport both horizontally and vertically in the logistics chain
Rule maker	New entrants in rail operations set/demand new rules with regard to, e.g., international train drivers licenses, internationally harmonized train control systems, maximum axle loads, etc.
Specialist	Players in international rail transport position themselves in the value chain and become specialists
Improver	Efficient rail transport services have been introduced. You could call the new players who do so improvers

Figure 16.1 Within this future, envision different roles of a player in the industry.

Let's examine how a railway company took the transport value chain and plotted where each different role player fit in.

From this analysis the company concluded that it was most comfortable as a game player, its current role. But the exercise made clear that if the company wanted to be in other positions of the value

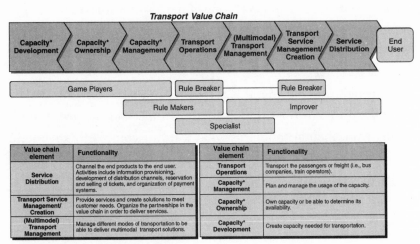

Value chain element	Functionality		Value chain element	Functionality
Service Distribution	Channel the end products to the end user. Activities include information provisioning, development of distribution channels, reservation and selling of tickets, and organization of payment systems.		Transport Operations	Transport the passengers or freight (i.e., bus companies, train operators).
			Capacity* Management	Plan and manage the usage of the capacity.
Transport Service Management/ Creation	Provide services and create solutions to meet customer needs. Organize the partnerships in the value chain in order to deliver services.		Capacity* Ownership	Own capacity or be able to determine its availability.
(Multimodel) Transport Management	Manage different modes of transportation to be able to deliver multimodal transport solutions.		Capacity* Development	Create capacity needed for transportation.

*Capacity: Land, Infrastructure, Rolling Stock, Terminals, People

Figure 16.2 Analyze the impact of each of the roles by relating them to your future industry.

chain, it had to change philosophies in some parts of its business or set up different companies next to them.

The components of this value chain make clear why this is so. *Capacity development* makes sure that all the resources needed to create transport are there, from preparation of land and infrastructure to rolling stock and people. *Capacity ownership* means the ownership of the rails and the trains running over them. *Capacity management* means making sure that the capacity remains available and is applied well, as in effective train scheduling. *Transport operations* is making sure the trains run on the track, when and where they are supposed to. *Multimodal transport management* means finding the means to move passengers or cargo from point A to point B by whatever means are most effective, including, perhaps, coach or truck. *Transport service creation* involves added services that supplement the actual transport. *Distribution of services* means making sure that the end user has access to these services.

The different roles identified here have "best fits" in different steps of the value chain. The game player, for example, fits best in the first three steps of the value chain, where rules are largely fixed by regulators and other parties. As a result, there's little room for rule breaking or rule making. An "Improver" (one of the possible roles of a player in the industry) would find little here to improve. In contrast, the Improver finds a more satisfying role closer to the end user, who will value new services.

Through role playing, this transport company came to understand the different roles that it might assume. This helped it break through the mental model of what kind of competitors it might expect, enabling the company to steer toward the desired future, increasing stability along the way.

CHAPTER 17

It's how you play the game

Game playing stretches thinking about what the rules are

G*ame playing* is a useful tool for understanding the action and reaction of whoever is out there, be they competitors or other influencers of your business results. Game playing stretches one's thinking about what the rules are and demonstrates that different people can have different interpretations of rules. It provides an understanding of what it takes to be successful in current and, perhaps, future games. Game playing also provides insight into how the rules can be changed, by permitting experimentation with the rules and with the assignments of different players. It allows you to determine what signals you should give to competitors and how to understand the signals that competitors give you. Game playing can also help you understand how situations can be created in which you and your competitor are both better off—a win-win scenario.

Far simpler game playing is available than that where computer modeling is used to predict and simulate competitors' actions and reactions. Start, for example, by thinking about children's games (Figure 17.1).

Two main differentiators in children's games are the number of phases within the game and whether people have different assignments. The simplest games have only one phase and all players have the same assignment. In the games "Ludo" and "Sorry," each player has the same assignment and does only two things: moves pieces ahead and tries to throw competitors off the board. In "Monopoly," all players have the same assignment, but the game has different phases:

- Buy the real estate until all the parcels are sold.
- Swap with competitors to obtain contiguous blocks.
- Build as many hotels as possible to hasten competitors' bankruptcy.

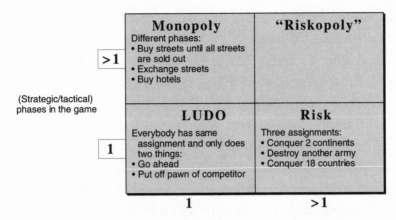

Figure 17.1 Understand the games to play.

In contrast, "Risk" has one phase but players may have different assignments. In Risk three assignments are possible: conquer two continents, destroy somebody else, or conquer 18 countries or more. You win by completing your special assignment before competitors complete their assignments.

We could not come up with a board game that has different phases and different assignments. But imagine it as a combination of Monopoly and Risk, which we call "Riskopoly." In this game you first have to buy streets or countries—as many as possible—and then occupy them. In the second phase you each have special assignments, perhaps to conquer a specific part of the world or to destroy a specific opponent.

Game playing in your industry is much like this. Take, for instance, a mobile telephone business. In the first phase, everybody tries to get as many licenses as possible all over the place. In the second phase (which in the real world has been going on for some time) people start exchanging the licenses or exchanging the shares that they own in different locations. In the next phase, players create competitive advantage by linking the mobile service to, for example, their fixed telecom assets. In fact, the rules of life are not so different from those of children's games.

In another case, you have only one phase but different assignments. The traditional telecom players saw their assignment as being the leader in a specific geographical area. Along came a new player, like Worldcom, which targeted not a specific geographical area but a specific market segment, such as the financial sector. Understanding this will help you get more insight into possible games that you, as well as your competitor, might play. It will help you to understand your assumptions about your industry's rules of the game.

How do you start game playing? Why not get in the mood by playing the children's games? That loosens everybody up. Then play a game based on one of the four basic types and tailor it to look like the game you play in your normal business life: adjust any rules and regulations and the name on the board to your specific industry. The first time you play, follow the rules. The second time you play, try to discover new possibilities within the rules. Form a secret partnership with your competitors, for example, to squeeze the player in front of or behind you in the value chain. Or form a secret partnership with players in front of or behind you in the value chain to squeeze competitors. Learn to use, and to abuse, the partners you make. This will teach you not to take the rules for granted any more.

How does all this help create stability? By breaking your mental model of the rules of the game in your industry (written and unwritten), this game playing should help you understand your assumptions about the basis of competition.

CHAPTER 18

Pattern recognition

Learning from other sectors

The *pattern recognition* tool is a way to learn a lesson from similar industries that are a step ahead in dealing with change. Pattern recognition clarifies the consequences and the speed of specific market developments. Performing this exercise helps you anticipate the consequences of different environmental changes. It gives you more insight into industry drivers and shows the successful and unsuccessful business models that can be found in similar industries. Because these changes are already happening elsewhere, no one can justifiably claim that such changes are impossible or doubt the speed at which they occur.

Let's see how pattern recognition works in the utility industry, using telecom as the similar industry that went through deregulation years earlier. In both industries, regulatory bodies have to ensure that fair competition exists in the market. How does a company demonstrate that? A significant share of the market needs to be in hands other than those of the traditional monopolist. If new competitors do not acquire sufficient market share, the regulators intervene, perhaps skewing regulations in favor of new competitors or to make sure that new competitors are added.

Before deregulation the incumbent telecom and utility companies each had all the customers, and whether they wanted the customers was irrelevant, because they had to serve all customers. The only objective they had was to try to increase the revenue from existing customers, and this was often precluded by regulated rates.

Deregulating the market affects many areas, especially customer care (Figure 18.1). An established company must adapt to the fact that it does not have all the customers, nor does it want all the customers. Therefore, it must learn to segment its customers and handle them differently: Acquire, reacquire, and retain customers you want, instead of serving everyone; release and discourage customers you don't want.

By recognizing a pattern of four phases in the telecom industry, the utility industry was better prepared for the consequences of the start of competition.

As shown in phase 1 in Figure 18.2, more than 2 years before the start of competition, the only thing incumbent companies cared about was increasing revenue (by acquiring new customers or selling more to existing customers). As competition neared in phase 2, customer retention came into play, and a lot of money could be made by doing this well because the existing customer base was so large.

As deregulation took hold, in phase 3, and competition came to the market, incumbents lost customers. Indeed, the regulatory body ensured that they lost customers in order to demonstrate the existence of an open market and fair competition. So releasing the right customers became important for incumbent players: A lot of money could be made by losing the unprofitable customers. Shedding them did not provoke the regulator, who could still point to the market share of the new competitor.

In phase 4, 2 years after the introduction of competition, reacquisition of lost but profitable customers (another major shift in customer-

	We have the customer	We do not have the customer
We want the customer	Retain the attractive customers and increase revenue	Acquire new customers Reacquire attractive customers who have been lost to competition
We don't want the customer	Release customers who add negative value to the competition	Discourage customers who do not add or add little or no value at all

Figure 18.1 Customer-care objectives change because of deregulation.

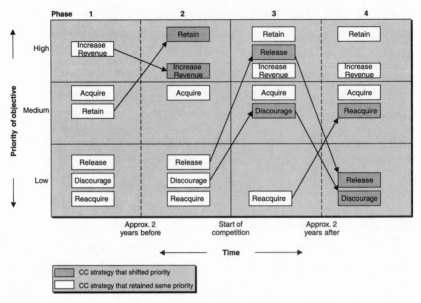

Figure 18.2 The priority shifts over time between the customer-care objectives related to the start of competition.

care priority) came into play. Releasing unprofitable customers had been completed by then.

By understanding the patterns of customer care in the telecom industry, the utility industry learned a good deal. For instance, the priorities and therefore the incentives for salespeople needed to shift within each phase (Figure 18.3).

This led to disruption among the people working there. When increasing revenue was the main priority, the major incentives for salespeople were to find additional customers or sell more to existing customers (both measured in sales figures). In the 2 years before competition, the retention program was started, and retention of attractive customers became top priority (measured not by sales but by customer satisfaction, a key indicator of brand loyalty). After the start of competition, the incentives were changed again to make sure that salespeople were rewarded for releasing unattractive customers and discouraged for acquiring unprofitable customers. When the

Customer-care priorities	• **Increase revenue** • **Acquire new customers**	• **Retain attractive customers** • **Increase revenue**	• **Retain attractive customers** • **Release unattractive customers**	• **Retain attractive customers** • **Increase revenue** • **Reacquire lost customers**
Consequences for Sales Department	• Understand customer needs and key processes • Focus on acquisition	Understand who are gold, silver, and bronze customers to retain most attractive • Build loyalty strategies	• Understand customer profitability to release least profitable ones	• Have a working, up-to-date database to know which to reacquire
Consequences for Sales Incentives	• Incentivize additional customers	• Disincentivize changes in customers (chum)	• Set targets according to net profitability • Punish keeping, acquiring unproftiable customers	• Incentivize overall net profit growth

Approx. 2 years before	Start of competition	Approx. 2 years after

Figure 18.3 This priority shift has major consequences for the way the sales department is run.

reacquisition of lost customers came into play, while retention of attractive customers remained important, salespeople needed to be given bonuses based on overall growth in net income.

Recognizing this pattern enabled utility companies to avoid the disruption that could have been caused by adapting to one new priority after another. Even though the major change in the utility industry had not yet appeared, utility companies were able, through pattern recognition, to foresee the impact of the coming turbulence and the actions needed. The sales department saw it could avoid disruption by ensuring that in every phase each objective (both high and low priority) had separate resources attached. The department could go from one phase to the next by changing the amount of the resources used, according to the level of priority. By applying this principle, the salespeople had consistent Enablers and Triggers over time, as the company used Bridging techniques.

CHAPTER 19

Navigating in the fog

Creating a "memory" of the future

The *scenario planning* tool exposes you to the impact of possible future outcomes of the uncertainties that surround you. This understanding of possible futures helps you to shape a robust action plan that takes into account different outcomes of the uncertainties. And that helps you understand the validity of your business model within the changing environment. It also creates in your management team a "memory of the future," which enables you to react immediately to indications that a particular scenario may be becoming reality. You learn to understand early warning signals of the probable occurrence of specific market changes, allowing you to build responses into your planning.

With scenario planning, the first thing you should do is to identify the uncertainties that worry you the most (Figure 19.1). Then paint a picture of the world under the different outcomes of these major uncertainties. After painting the picture, try to explain the different possible futures and test the strategic options in each of them. Based on these, select the optimal strategy (Figure 19.2). Finally, embed this scenario thinking into your company and monitor for early warning signals.

How do you identify the most worrying uncertainty? You tap into as many sources as possible—and a key source is the "gut feeling" of your management. You assess these uncertainties by their impact on your company. You try to figure out the assumptions of your business strategy and identify whether they are sound or based on thin ice.

Let's consider the scenario development of a fictitious satellite communications company named Satcom. One key uncertainty is whether the base product will involve differentiation or commoditization. Another is whether the market will be stable or will be absorbed.

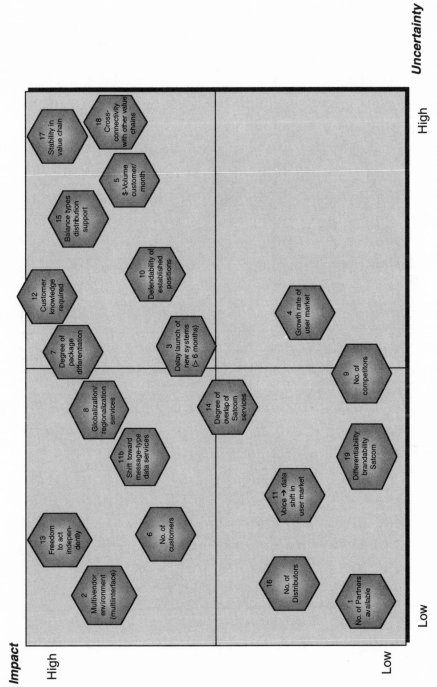

Figure 19.1 Identify the most worrying uncertainties.

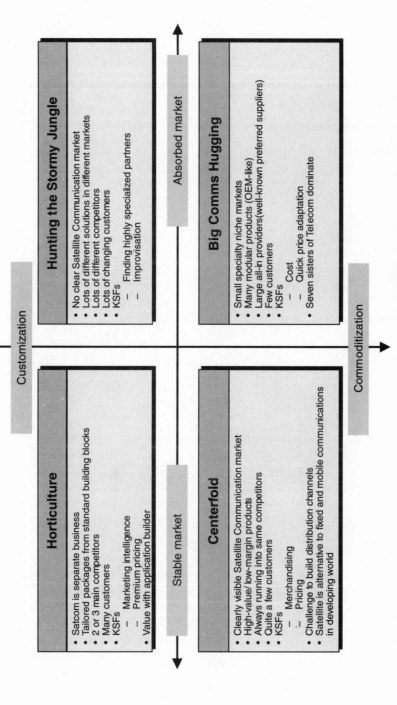

Horticulture

- Satcom is separate business
- Tailored packages from standard building blocks
- 2 or 3 main competitors
- Many customers
- KSFs
  - Marketing intelligence
  - Premium pricing
- Value with application builder

Hunting the Stormy Jungle

- No clear Satellite Communication market
- Lots of different solutions in different markets
- Lots of different competitors
- Lots of changing customers
- KSFs
  - Finding highly specialized partners
  - Improvisation

Centerfold

- Clearly visible Satellite Communication market
- High-value/low-margin products
- Always running into same competitors
- Quite a few customers
- KSFs
  - Merchandising
  - Pricing
- Challenge to build distribution channels
- Satellite is alternative to fixed and mobile communications in developing world

Big Comms Hugging

- Small specialty niche markets
- Many modular products (OEM-like)
- Large all-in providers(well-known preferred suppliers)
- Few customers
- KSFs
  - Cost
  - Quick price adaptation
- Seven sisters of Telecom dominate

Customization

Commoditization

Absorbed market

Stable market

Figure 19.2 Paint the pictures of the world under each of the different outcomes of the most worrying uncertainties.

144

Should the absorbed market become reality, and commoditization take hold, small specialty niche markets would result. The company would need many modular products and large all-inclusive providers. That's a totally different business environment from a situation where customization and a stable market became the reality. Satcom would stay a separate business there, with tailored packages from standard building blocks. The whole market dynamic would be totally different.

Scenarios tend to be given graphic names. Satcom called the customization/stable market scenario *Horticulture.* The other three environments were:

Big Comms Hugging, with the few big companies dominating but cooperating in this market.

Hunting the Stormy Jungle, a market with many different solutions, competitors, and customers, where it is hard to look more than a few feet ahead.

Centerfold, a stable and commoditized market that is clearly visible and transparent, with lots of customers.

Once you have identified these scenarios, you can determine what the optimal strategy is. After selecting the optimal strategy for each scenario, see if there is one that is robust under all possible outcomes of the future. Satcom found that partnering with several other satellite communications companies was a good idea, whatever the future.

With scenario thinking, the company was able to remain stable in a very uncertain environment, by selecting a robust strategy. Understanding the impact of the uncertainties allowed it to prepare for and understand the risks and impacts of the selected strategies.

Because the company knew what the possible futures were, it knew which early warning signals to look for. Should it spot an early warning signal, it could decide which path to follow. All the action plans were rehearsed, by discussions during the scenario exercise, so the company was able to move much faster than its competitors. It also understood which decisions had to be delayed to decrease the level of disruption. As an added benefit, it was able to understand where to make modest investments in what might turn out to be golden opportunities.

CHAPTER 20

Different tools, different toolboxes

Each stability structure applies strategic tools differently

A s noted previously, each of the four stability structures applies the strategic tools differently to foresee turbulence.

The Pyramid applies the tools on a yearly basis to foresee environmental changes far in advance, enabling incremental innovation. *Nightmare competitor* exercises are applied to identify potential process improvements and ways in which they can influence their environment. *Role playing* is applied to understand, well in advance, which role to play, and how to move slowly and steadily toward it. It also provides an opportunity to choose a role that avoids big changes. *Game playing* is applied to foresee turbulence driven by competitive action and to determine ways to influence the environment so that it will not be necessary to change. *Pattern recognition* is used to plan the Pyramid's incremental changes. *Scenario planning* is used to define a strategy that makes it unnecessary to change too often.

A Cube also applies the tools on a yearly basis, enabling it to plan and time the periods of calm and transition it needs. *Nightmare competitor* not only helps to identify the turbulence but also to understand the least disruptive way of going through the transition, by identifying what a best-in-class structure would do in the "after-transition" phase. *Role playing* is applied to energize the staff for the coming transition, by focusing on their ambitions. *Game playing,* as well as *pattern recognition* and *scenario planning,* are used to understand what the appropriate transitions are and to make sure that each is planned for and timed appropriately. *Pattern recognition* and *scenario planning* can help to understand when to start the transition.

The main application of the tools in the Cylinder is to identify the repetitive events and incremental improvement possibilities. The tools are applied more often than in the Pyramid or Cube, and in a much more flexible way, putting less pressure on resources. *Nightmare competitor* is used to identify potential process improvements. *Role playing* is applied to motivate people working in the Cylinder cycle to strive to become the very best. *Pattern recognition* is one of the strongest tools to identify repetitive events because it forecasts the pattern of changes in the environment. *Game playing* and *scenario planning* provide understanding of whether the Cylinder needs to adapt its dimension of flexibility.

In the Sphere, the tools are applied to broaden the portfolio of initiatives, increasing the odds of having a winner in the portfolio. *Nightmare competitor* helps to identify the initiative that could be taken by competitors. It also helps to improve the process of creating and developing initiatives and in taking account of examples from other industries. *Role playing* is used to motivate people to capture whatever golden opportunity might be out there. *Game playing* is especially useful to understanding the playing field, increasing the odds of capturing necessary initiatives. *Pattern recognition* is used by the Sphere to predict the odds of different initiatives in the portfolio. And *scenario planning* is applied to identify and capture the possible golden opportunity in one of the possible futures. It also helps balance the portfolio of initiatives over the different possible futures.

For strategy to be realized, connections must be built to the real, operational world. Tactics provide those connections, and that's what we'll take up in Chapter 21.

Ferrying between thinking and doing

Tactics translate strategic goals into usable targets

Tactics are like a ferry, carrying the necessary learning from strategic thinking to operations and back. Without bridges, strategy has little chance to steer the organization and help it deal with turbulence. Without ferries, organizations must handle turbulence without strategic priority setting and without operational references. This often leads to nonaligned behavior, a form of shooting from the hip. To create stability, it's absolutely crucial to build bridges. Tactics are those bridges.

Consider, for example, the construction of a house. Unless the construction workers are instructed by the architect, it's unlikely that the final building will look anything like the original drawings. If the architect doesn't visit and examine the site before creating the drawings, it's possible the underpinnings will not be adequate to support the building envisioned. Good coordination between the architect and the construction workers is essential—the ferries between them create stability and avoid disruption.

The key strategic activities in an organization are to set the goals, understand the constraints, and apply the company values. The key tactical activities are to translate the strategic goals into usable targets, to weigh the options, and to apply the resources. Tactics must also settle on a plan with a specific measurable goal that is realistic and timely. This, in turn, drives the operations. The key operational activities are to decide on resource allocation and to decide on timing, and then, in the feedback loop, to deliver a status report that lets the people in tactics know what the reality is. In tactics they must digest this reality and explain its impact to the people in strategy. So tactics ferries between strategy and operations.

The form the connection should take depends on the stability structure. In each stability structure, the focus is different:

In the *Pyramid* tactical activities are aimed at controlling operations and ensuring incremental adjustments. Strategic, tactical, and operational activities are organized relatively separately.

In the *Cube* success depends on understanding the transitions and on how well you are able to cope with the unknown during the transitions.

In the *Cylinder* the main role of tactical activities is to provide learning between strategy and operations, ensuring that the Cylinder rolls on smoothly.

In the *Sphere* strategy, tactics and operations are more or less integrated to ensure that the right operational decisions can be made and action taken on the spot. Time cannot be wasted.

The contribution to stability is also different for each structure:

In a *Pyramid* the distance between strategic thinking and operational activity is great. Tactics ensures that the Pyramid is able to handle potentially huge barriers incrementally, by providing a continuous bridge for constant information exchange.

In a *Cube* tactical activities are closely linked to strategic thinking between transitions. During transitions, tactical activities are steering operations. In times of rest, the ferry remains at the strategic bank; in times of transition, at the operational bank.

In the *Cylinder* tactics help to ensure that the experiences and lessons from previous cycles are incorporated in managing future cycles.

In the *Sphere*, there's no time to do things twice and no time to investigate each opportunity thoroughly before work commences on it. Tactical activities are designed to help make the good decisions outnumber the bad ones to provide as much of an overview as possible, to finish promising projects in spite of organizational barriers, and to ensure that if you have a winning horse, you never lose.

A lack of proper tactics creates specific disruptions in each structure:

In a *Pyramid,* the lack of tactical coordination can cause a complete mismatch between objectives and results. Without such a bridge, everybody can think they're doing the right things while nothing is achieving the desired results.

In a *Cube,* without tactics you might choose the wrong reason and the wrong moment to start the transition phase. This can limit the potential Surging capabilities and be massively disruptive should the transition prove to be unnecessary.

In the *Cylinder,* lack of tactics can lead to operational errors repeated again and again.

In the *Sphere,* a lack of proper tactics can turn the structure into an unguided missile, with options determined only by chance.

Managing tactics ensures that the strategic choices are followed and translated into understandable language for operations. It basically takes four steps to manage tactics:

1. Interpret and translate the strategic plan into understandable language. What guidelines do you want to run the company by? What specific ambitions does the company want to realize? What values does the company want to live by? What financial constraints has the company set for itself? What is the scope of the business? What things do we do and what things don't we do? What is the medium-term direction of the company?

2. Guide and support the day-to-day operations. What are the decisions that people in operations can make? What boundaries are people in operations never allowed to cross?

3. Monitor day-to-day practice and control day-to-day operations in order to uncover quickly any unexpected deviations. People need to be able to understand the unexpected, whether it is the unexpected activities undertaken by the organization of the

company, the differences between what is said and what is *done* in operations, or the unexpected reaction of the market and people outside your company.

4. Report developments that influence goals and decisions in the medium and long term and provide feedback to strategic thinking. It's important to understand when to raise a red flag and when not to.

In many ways the umbrella of managing tactics is a tool in itself. Of the many specific tools you might employ in addition, we want to look closely at three because we think they add considerably to stability:

- *Structured idea management* helps to uncover hidden existing knowledge and facilitate collective new thinking by generating ideas and developing them into an action plan.
- *Risk management* helps to identify the roadblocks, assess their impact, and determine the way around them.
- *Contingency planning* describes for a specific risk that you cannot manage the actions that should be taken when the risk occurs.

We'll take them up in the following chapters.

CHAPTER 22

Understanding the tactical tools

Three ways to sharpen critical thinking

*S*tructured *idea management* helps to uncover hidden existing knowledge and to facilitate collective new thinking by generating ideas and developing them into an action plan in a seven-step process (Figure 22.1). By carefully selecting the participants, management can cross the natural border between strategy-oriented and operations-oriented people. This has the side effect of getting people to think about the direction of the company and how to get there, creating enthusiasm, motivation, and self-confidence. And these are all necessary to make the plan work. In a later stage, during the roll-out of an implementation plan, a recurring brainstorming session can help find new solutions and rethink the old ones. If done well, people will like it a lot. In fact, they'll do it themselves, training other people in structured idea management, so the tool will spread rapidly through the company.

Start with a small number of people who select the criteria and prepare a brainstorm briefing document. For the first brainstorming session, invite people from different backgrounds. Done right, this session should produce roughly 150 ideas from many perspectives. In step 3, a smaller group drawn from the larger one divides the ideas into 10 to 15 clusters. In step 4, the original large group examines the clusters, trying to find ways to enrich the ideas—with more detail, sharper thinking, and so on. This not only produces better ideas but also gets everyone involved, which results in better motivation to continue the work. In step 5, the smaller group ranks the different concepts in terms of importance and attractiveness. In step 6, the small group creates a final ranking and picks two to three concepts to go with. In step 7, an action plan is created to implement the strategy and to allow for quick wins.

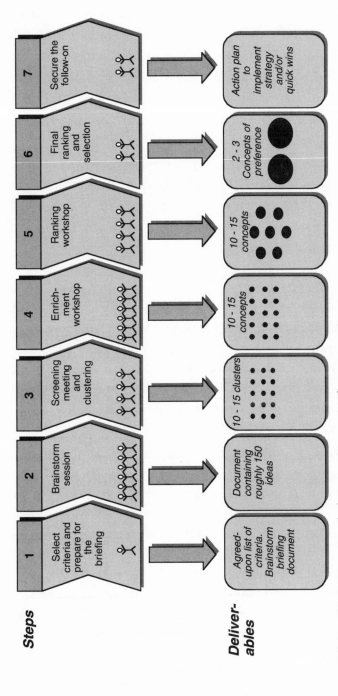

Figure 22.1 Structured idea management takes seven steps.

An essential part of this process is the selection of the participants, ensuring that both strategy-oriented and operations-oriented people are included. This allows people to look both at their own turf and at the other side of the company, bridging the gap between strategy and operations. In the sequence of steps, the strategic people and the operational people complement each other and create a feeling of shared responsibility and shared vision.

Risk management is the key to making choices in a world where priorities constantly shift at the same time that decisions have to be made. Risk management involves three steps: identify the roadblocks, assess their impact, and determine the way around them. Let's look at each in turn (Figure 22.2):

1. *Inventorize the things you are sure you know:* You identify the issues that you know about, creating an inventory of things you're sure you know. Go carefully through the strategy and play the devil's advocate. The most obvious and probable risks can be assessed. Question all assumptions. Analyze key success factors to determine killer risks. Take a critical look at projects and plans that have failed in the past to make sure that learning takes place and that you don't make the same mistake twice.

2. *Reveal the unknown future:* You recognize that there are some issues you know you don't know about, so you try to reveal this future. A nightmare competitor workshop can provide insights into how the best-in-class player would handle the unknown future. The workshop can also allow you to ask on what foundation you would build your company if you were starting from scratch, with all you've learned. If you realize that the best-in-class player would take certain actions in a certain environment and you would not be able to, at least you've discovered that you know that you don't know. Doomsday-thinking sessions can help you discover what went wrong and what could have been done differently. "We went bankrupt," you might begin. Well, why? If

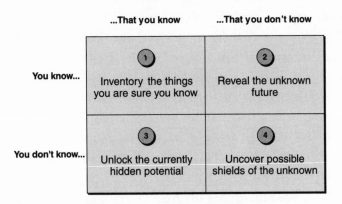

Figure 22.2 The matrix to identify your blind spots.

you can answer that question, perhaps you can determine that there are certain things you don't know . . . and now you'll know that you don't know. In some cases, you can create the future by defining rules. Not everything should be reactive; you can actively set some conditions of the future, increasing the chance that things that happen are not in an area where you don't know how to react. You can take action where the costs of regret are too high: If you have to invest a certain amount of money and you can't calculate the outcome, but losing or missing the opportunity would be a billion-dollar problem . . . well, take the risk. The cost of regret is too high.

3. *Unlock the currently hidden potential:* You discover issues that you didn't know you knew about, unlocking hidden potential. Again use a doomsday session. Suddenly you discover unrealized hidden potential within your team. You can use structured idea management techniques to amplify each other's knowledge and learning. Use pattern recognition and system-thinking techniques to uncover risks collectively that individually would remain hidden. Use the potential of the whole team, not just the potential of each member.

4. *Uncover possible shields of the unknown:* You find issues that you didn't know you didn't know about. This reveals to you the knowledge that you don't know something. It's absolutely crucial from time to time to ask outsiders to come in and to "shoot holes" in your risk management to check your own thinking. Constantly question a culture of comfort because the one thing you can be sure of is that you cannot be sure of everything. In the end, as Andrew Grove of Intel likes to say, only the paranoid survive.

Once you have identified the roadblocks, assess their impact by three measures. You want to determine the chance of occurrence, the likely damage, and the estimated time of impact (Figure 22.3).

Chance of occurrence can range from "you can bet on it" to "plan for it" to "you never know." You need to try to get a feeling of what the probability is. The likely damage should be categorized as high, medium, or low. Try to work out whether arrival is imminent, a way off but getting closer, or far in the distance.

Plotting risks in three dimensions (as shown in Figure 22.3) allows you to manage a portfolio of risks. Most projects in most companies

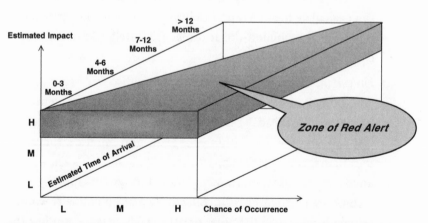

Figure 22.3 Assessing the red-alert zone consists of calculating chance of occurrence, estimating the "damage it will do," and estimating the time of arrival.

we've worked with manage risk by dealing with those that have high impact and a high chance of occurrence in the coming 3 months— basically a 0- to 3-month red-alert zone. With the complete portfolio of risks, you can focus on those risks with high potential impact and a likely chance of occurrence looking farther ahead, perhaps 12 months.

Let's say that Risk 1 is 12 months ahead. Its estimated impact is medium, as is the likelihood of occurrence. In the risk cube, Risk 1 is *not* at the moment in the red-alert zone, and so nobody in the company is paying any attention. But let's say that as Risk 1 gets closer, 6 months out, you determine through impact analysis that it is likely, even certain, that it will hit you, with high impact. By paying attention now and tracking the risk, you might be able to take action to avoid or mitigate Risk 1 before it even reaches the red-alert zone.

The last step in managing risk is to determine the way ahead, most especially for those risks in the red-alert zone. You have two choices: you can either break down the risk into manageable parts by making plans to reduce its impact or you make plans to reduce the chance of occurrence. Where neither choice will work, you make contingency plans.

A contingency plan provides a description of a specific risk, the way it will influence the business in several distinctive scenarios, and the actions that should be taken when the event occurs. Contingency plans are crucial for "binary risks," events that can flip either way, where you are either completely successful or completely unsuccessful. When you pick certain risks and build a contingency for a certain moment, you create a time line of happenings with the desired outcome. During that time, you constantly answer the question "What if . . . ?" It's crucial to find the right balance between underestimating a risk and overestimating.

A contingency plan is always aimed at reducing a specific risk along the axes: minimizing the impact, delaying the time of arrival, or reducing the chance of occurrence. But you want to keep the plan simple, and you want to use all the knowledge built up in the previous phases before you decided a plan was needed. A crucial part of contingency planning involves human resources. You want to make absolutely sure that you have the right people in house when the event occurs. Don't overcommit your best entrepreneurs elsewhere because you'll need them in these cases. You'll also want to carefully build strategic supplier alliances so you can depend on your suppliers when you need them.

CHAPTER 23

How one telecom used the tools

Tactics in action: a case study

N ow that we've identified some tools, let's see how they serve a European telecom operator that needed to change its position from monopolist to market player. The telecommunications industry was being redefined in several ways. Globalization was forcing the company to compete in new markets; indeed, it was redefining the markets. Privatization of former monopolies led to a reduced role for government; liberalization and deregulation stimulated a competitive environment. Four technological developments also stimulated competition—digitization, the increased use of fiber optics, the introduction of mobile communications, and most recently the growing role of the Internet.

The company itself was going through major changes. Historically a state-owned company, in the 1990s it was privatized and offered shares to the public. Competition grew from fragmented in the early 1990s to modest in the mid-1990s to full competition by the end of the decade. Massive reorganization was needed to adapt to this competitive environment and to the technological changes taking place. A new management was installed. The corporate culture had to adapt to all these new circumstances. To succeed amid all this change, the company needed effective tactics:

1. To grow considerably in the business-to-business market, the company needed to manage tactics.

2. Confronted with the enormous opportunity of the interactive market, the company used structured idea management to generate new ideas.

3. Risk management was used to cope with major infrastructure change projects.

4. Contingency plans enabled the company to respond to competition in the mobile market.

Managing Tactics. As the changes took effect, the company's clients became more and more international, and the company was no longer able to deliver everything that was asked for. Competition increased which led to price pressure, a loss of market share, and slower growth of demand. New technologies threatened. Each year initiatives were started to develop products and services, but there was no continuity in these efforts, and the gap between strategy and operations remained. The company knew it had to develop a new portfolio, but didn't know how to. On top of that resources were becoming scarce. Making the right decisions became crucial.

With strictly defined limitations, the company decentralized decision making on allocation of resources. It set apart its "large businesses" unit to manage tactics in this specific area. The company strategy was translated into an implementation plan that was updated every 6 months through the combined effort of operational people, the management of the business unit, and the strategy unit of the company.

In the end the company was able to cope with the constant change in a flexible and profitable manner. Belief in the company's management increased. Customers and their needs were segmented, an approach that could be used in strategy, tactical, and operational levels and was accepted by everyone involved. This enabled the development of a new portfolio that could be offered to the company's most important customers. The structured approach to the development of this portfolio also enabled the company to target other potential customers more directly. And once the whole process was in place, the company was able to make decisions concerning the portfolio much more quickly.

Structured Idea Management. Competition was gradually increasing in the interactive market, and the company's business unit needed to deal with this threat. Most ideas for new products were initiated by the manager, and those coming from the organization were neglected. Because of a mismatch in strategic input and operational experience, only very long-term and very short-term projects were initiated. The most profitable products were nearly mature and the business unit could not rely on those for the future.

By installing structured idea management, the business unit was able to increase commitment and align its strategic and operational efforts. Based on the strategic plans, targets were set that were directly related to the necessary changes in the portfolio. Management had to agree on these targets, enabling other employees to generate ideas aimed at fulfilling them without further interference. By putting together people from different parts of the business unit in a risk-free environment, many more ideas were generated. A sense of shared ownership and responsibility increased people's commitment significantly.

As a result the business unit was rationalized and was able to run its operations in a profitable manner. Corporate management was convinced of the need to get people from all parts of the company involved in the development process. The business unit was able to generate and develop ideas and implement them into profitable products. The need for profitability, and the responsibility for achieving this, was firmly fixed in everyone's mind.

Risk Management. The introduction of number portability was an enormously complex challenge. Telecom operators had to follow regulations and take care of the installment of number portability. Although the objective of the project was clear, implementation was barely manageable. The apparent distance between different parts of the organization created communications problems.

Risk management involving operational and strategic people enabled the company to structure the approach and to set priorities. To identify risks, several sessions were set up involving strategic people, operational people, and external people, as well as experts on the particular issues at hand. This process resulted in a complete view of all the perceived risks within the organization—an eye-opener for almost everyone involved. Frequent risk-monitoring sessions attended by representatives of all the subprojects enabled a categorization of the risks, and this provided important input for the weekly management meetings. The chair of these risk-monitoring sessions was the overall project manager, which further increased people's commitment to risk management.

As a result, risks were handled by the appropriate people, enabling a much more efficient approach. Real problems were identified in time. The frequent monitoring of risks enabled the organization to plan specific actions to take away the threat. Risks that could not be handled immediately were passed on to management, which decided on further action. Communication improved and the insights gained into the overall complexity of the project facilitated the effective handling of risks.

Contingency Plans. The mobile business unit faced fresh competition, which raised a number of issues. The business unit knew it was not fully prepared; it had no clear view on what the competition was planning to do, in what ways it wanted to enter the market, what pricing strategy it would follow, and what positioning it would take in its marketing strategy. It did not know how the distribution channels would react. It did not know what pieces of the distribution chain would prefer competitors. It didn't have the slightest idea how customers would respond to the new competition. Faced with all these unknowns, the business unit wanted to be able to pursue its objectives actively rather than reacting to competitors' moves.

A contingency plan was developed to prepare for all possible steps by competitors. The plan was built first by generating all combinations of possible actions and reactions of the competition, the distribution channels, and the customers. These combinations were developed into several possible futures. And these were simulated to determine what actions were needed to go forward successfully. A list of outcome-independent and outcome-dependent actions was created based on these simulations.

The resulting contingency plan enabled the management of the business unit to reach all its objectives, regardless of what the competition might do. Actions were based on the goals and the objectives of the business unit, not on what competitors would do. The business unit was optimally prepared for possible competitive moves. Confidence levels were high because all possible competitive moves had been seen in the simulations. When the competition entered the market, the business unit was able to respond quickly and remain the strong market leader. When the competition placed a strong emphasis on marketing, for example, the business unit, prepared from the simulations, was able to profit smartly from its competitors' efforts. Rather than starting a huge campaign of its own to promote mobile communications, the company let its rival promote the service, increasing public awareness, and remained confident its own position as market leader would draw customers. When competitors cut prices sharply, the business unit followed, but in a deliberate fashion, without panicking. In the end this produced higher margins with only a slight loss of market share.

This particular telecommunications company was but one of many organizations that have responded smartly to competitive threats with tactical tools. As we noted previously, these diverse tools need to be applied differently in each stability structure.

CHAPTER 24

Applying tactical tools to the structures

As always, each structure requires a different approach

Within the *Pyramid*, tactics must emphasize perfection, so structured idea management, risk management, and contingency planning are important. Feedback, and thus managing tactics, is aimed at controlling operations to attain the desired perfection. Managing tactics brings thought and action together, which can be especially hard in a Pyramid, that most rigid of stability structures. Structured idea management provides a good, essential platform to bring the normally highly separated strategy and operations people together.

Structured idea management should be carried out when the strategic plan has been finalized. Because the process of determining risks and making contingency plans is quite rigid, this creative process is very welcome. By selecting people from strategy as well as operations, maximum synergy is achieved. A full report on risks, including chance of occurrence, damage done, time of arrival, and the names of the people responsible must be updated regularly. The contingency planning is attached directly to the risk management report, and the same level of detail is required. Contingency plans are carried out by line management but coordinated by the same person responsible for keeping track of the risk. Managing tactics has a controlling function: The team has to keep information on risks and contingencies up to date, and it must meet regularly with stakeholders, strategy makers, and external people to be able to adjust the course of action when necessary.

In a *Cube*, the large difference between the periods of relative calm and the periods of transition defines how tactics are used. The former is a time for preparation, while in periods of transition managing tactics plays a very important role in steering the operations. Important choices and decisions that cannot be made during periods of calm have to be made under pressure. An organization cannot risk chaos by leaving those decisions to the people in charge of operations. You can prepare meticulously, and you have to, so that once the transition starts you're able to make the right decisions at the right moment. Structured idea management is essential, and people from all parts of the company and even some outsiders must be involved in this exercise. This creates a competitive edge and is one of the few ways to prepare for things you don't know anything about. Risk management has to be carried out in detail and focuses on the transition stage because the transition is unpredictable. This has to be a creative process. A full report on risks is needed, and it is very important to use every possible way of identifying risks, because the Cube undergoes unpredictable transitions and risks are common. Contingency planning is done for all risks but only on headlines: Planning in too much detail is unwise because of the unpredictability of the identified risks. Managing tactics is the absolute key for success. All the preparation is useless if it is not used to steer operations. Because it is impossible to prepare for everything, the key decisions have to be made during, not before, operations.

Contingency planning has to focus on who rather than what. Because it is hard to predict anything at all, it is hard to specify what actions to take. That makes it even more necessary to be able to make decisions and make them quickly when things go wrong. During periods of calm, managing tactics has a controlling function just like in the Pyramid. During transitions, everything is aimed at making the right decisions fast. Preparation in a Cube is like a puzzle with lots of pieces missing. During transition, these pieces will be found one by one. The presence of top managers in the team ensures adequate decision power.

In the *Cylinder,* the learning process is embedded in the organization itself because the people are very experienced. The emphasis is on keeping informed about operations; the tactical process steers operations only incrementally. This leads to optimal efficiency, by nature an iterative process. Although the feedback loop incorporated in managing tactics ideally suits the needs of the Cylinder, tactics as a whole play a modest role in this structure. The key words are *efficiency* and *learning*, and everything is geared toward smoothing current and future cycles by learning from past cycles and adjusting to the lessons learned. Structured idea management is of minor importance for tactics because everybody knows what they are doing and not many new situations will be encountered. Risk management is distinctive within a Cylinder because not many new risks will be identified but the likelihood of occurrence and the time of arrival can be adjusted to the lessons learned. Contingency planning is fairly static, changing only when past experience proves contingencies wrong. Contingency plans are kept by the involved line managers and are updated at the end of each cycle. It is very important to allocate responsibilities for the contingencies to the same people responsible for normal operations.

Managing tactics is aimed primarily at control, but it also plays an important role in ensuring that the lessons learned and the changing external and internal conditions influence the current cycle. Managing tactics is carried out directly by top management. Optimization of the cycle is the most important aspect of tactics. Although changes to the cycle will be incremental by nature, they have to be put in place rigorously to work.

The *Sphere,* from a tactical point of view, is a special situation. In a Sphere, it is not much use specifying all the possible risks; contingency planning is very limited; detailed feedback of the operation is less important. Because it can stifle creativity, preparation is not desirable. On the other hand, managing tactics plays a crucial role because it is the only way to steer the decision-making process: Managing tactics is the de facto steering mechanism. Decisions have to be made ad hoc, based on the present situation of the Sphere. There is limited time for debate. Managing tactics is geared toward complete integration of strategy and operation. The ideal situation would be a sort of controlled big bang, when a framework applies to each process that takes place without interfering with spontaneity and creativity. Structured idea management is not used for translating the strategy into an implementation, but it can be used to chart all possible scenarios that might influence the running projects. A Sphere thrives on risk-taking risk. Only major risks that influence the company as a whole should be taken into account, so risk management on a detailed level is limited. Contingencies are rare within initiatives of the Sphere. If something goes wrong, you concentrate on building a new project instead of cleaning up the mess.

And now we must ferry across to Operations, where we will spend the next few chapters.

CHAPTER 25

Focusing on the destination

How Operations help to maintain stability

O perations ensure that the routes that maximize stability are followed. Operations are relevant to stability not the least because of a notorious incongruity that exists at many companies—and drains millions of dollars from them. While in theory everybody knows the importance of Operations, in fact operational management is rarely an important topic on the management agenda. The many management concepts in Operations are easy to grasp and quickly understood. Most business people have mastered the concepts, especially those who have had a career in Operations and are now in charge. Yet at the many companies we visit and consult with, we see a different reality—not many people operate by the principles they understand so well. We see Operations that suffer from overly rigid change planning. Employees work under stress, objectives are often not achieved on time, organizations grow increasingly inflexible, and budgets are exceeded. And all of these collectively cause a lot of Turbulence. We believe that truly excellent Operations create Stability.

Well-executed Operations help spot Stability threats at the earliest possible moment. They help manage the necessary level of detail of work. Properly implemented, they ensure that necessary activities are carried out in a timely fashion. And they ensure that resources—human, financial, or technological—are used efficiently.

In the *Pyramid,* Operations maintain Stability by continuously realizing incremental improvements in the most efficient and effective way. In the *Cube,* Operations allow for reliable milestones and concrete deliverables in periods of calm, and they ensure quick transitions in times of change. Operations also ensure robustness of the operational processes while going through the transition. In a *Cylinder,* Operations minimize disruption by executing detailed planning for each individual cycle, and they ensure the proper steering of the overall movement. In the *Sphere,* Operations reduce disruption by keeping as many options as possible open with the lowest possible investment, while at the same time continuing the most stable route forward.

Let's take a closer look at each of these.

In the *Pyramid,* Operations ensure that highly detailed plans are created and maintained. They allow for accurate training and empowerment of people within the appropriate boundaries of their roles and time frame. Operations coordinate consistent communications and incorporate incremental improvements into the day-to-day business. They monitor progress and performance continuously, providing people with psychological comfort. And they continuously align the organization and reduce the impact of unexpected events.

In a *Cube,* Operations provide reliable main milestones instead of detailed planned activities, for both the transition and the calm. They ensure up-front investment in fallbacks and agreed deliverables. For the people involved they ensure change readiness and preparation for change. Critical points are managed; organizations are aligned in transition; and calm people leading the transition are empowered. Operations also challenge the organization not to refreeze, allowing for more rapid responses when necessary. They show people that a transition will not last forever. By implementing radar screens, the continuity of the key processes can be monitored and the transition can be steered.

In a *Cylinder,* Operations facilitate and ensure new applications—that is, copying—of successful cycle competencies. They prevent frequent changes from disrupting the whole, and they build repetitive changes into the processes in a planned, controlled way. They ensure that the overall long-term direction and objectives of the company are met. And they build common denominators of change into the organization, creating and maintaining a library of plans and files of successful cycle operations of the past. This provides people with the confidence that "we're all running hard, but the direction is okay."

In a *Sphere*, Operations empower people to go for specific results and provide the maximum opportunity for people to experiment in a controlled way. Operations are particularly important in continuously identifying and stopping redundant options. They design the most stable route forward and indicate opportunities that need support. They guide leaders to the places where the most value can be added. They match the expected end results of different options and spot synergies and ensure the incorporation of lessons learned in the past. Operations also control investments and keep track of overall success and hit rates. They help management to select the most stable solutions over time and develop ways to reward successful failures. Finally, Operations keep risk levels acceptable so the company's future is not endangered.

Many specific operational tools create and enhance stability. The common denominator of all of them is they keep management well informed, helping management to identify key roadblocks and to respond with an appropriate set of actions. We will focus on four tools:

1. *Radar screens* scan and monitor crucial standardized information, using an intelligence network within the company.

2. The *war room* detects potential danger, alerts management to threats, and suggests possible solutions for operations.

3. *Adapting to stay on course* helps management to implement and carry out a responsive strategy by refining plans and organization.

4. *Rapid response capability,* the most spectacular tool, minimizes turbulence when the unexpected happens and allows management to adapt rigorously.

Close interaction between the tools is essential. Radar screens provide the main input for the war room, where skilled people use detailed knowledge (in the form of analyzed data) to find barriers and to alert management in time, and to plan responses. The preferred response, when time, budget, and people's stress levels permit, is to refine plans and refine the organization. But if quick change is necessary or unavoidable, the rapid response capability can be launched as a last resort. In the coming chapters, we'll look at each of these tools in turn.

CHAPTER 26

Radar screens

Keeping track of threats is essential

I magine that you're taking your family on a driving holiday to the south of France. "Radar screens" are crucial to get you there safely. During strategic planning, you chose Cannes as your destination. In Tactics, you planned and prepared for your trip. Now, in Operations, you get into the car, start the engine, and hit the road. To get there safely—indeed, to get there at all—it's crucial to know at all times what is going on around you. If you don't keep track of the road, your trip will end at the first turn. If you don't keep track of road signs, you might experience a huge delay before you reach your destination. If you don't control your speed, your trip may become significantly more expensive than you had budgeted for. If you don't rest adequately, you risk making mistakes and endangering your family. If you don't persuade your children to buy into your plan by continuously reminding them how great things will be once you're there and how much progress you're making toward the destination, they'll rebel and fight all the way. So the threats include delays, human resource issues, skills, the size of the staff, the budget, and more. Keeping track of these threats is crucial if you are to reach your destination. Radar screens provide essential information relevant to Operations. In this case, the radar screens are the front windshield, the speedometer, the clock, and the noise level in the backseat.

To build radar screens, three things need to be done.

The first is to define the type of radar screens that you need to install and select the target.

To define the types of radar screens that will be installed, determine the key threats for the part of the organization. We have identified 10 key threats.

Shortage of time can occur because of regulatory issues, changes in competition, the timing of related projects and initiatives, and more.

These create pressure for fast implementation. A *shortage of people and skills* can occur when unexpected events, even a calamity, pull people from parts of the organization, especially those parts where stability initiatives are carried out. A *shortage of money or a change in budget* can come about from unanticipated expenses or overspending at the front end. In a more extreme form, the management might order a 40 percent reduction in a budget to make its year-end results look nicer. *Changes in program scope* need to be monitored to make sure they do not turn into threats to stability. Another threat *is uncertainty in the environment*. An organization might be confronted with pressure from customer groups, which have specific ideas and specific requirements that require a program to change in midstream. *Change in opponents and sponsors* along the route. If people don't care for having critical resources withdrawn from their parts of the organization, that type of situation can create stress, tension, and opposition within the organization. *Conflict in stakeholder needs* can happen when benefits are taken away or when people suffer because other people get credit that the first group thinks were undeserved. As a result, people start putting pressure on your activities. The eighth stability threat is *disruption from other initiatives* on the program. *Breakdown of key processes* can result from the change program. And finally, *misalignment of Enablers and Triggers* can result in hot spots of change fatigue.

After the threats are identified, select the key indicators that affect planning and progress; determine the workload, functionality, and spirit of the people involved; measure conditions that may increase foreseen expenditures; and show the need to adapt communication. Then, based on the key threats and the indicators selected, set the time intervals between measurements. If turbulence is high, use shorter intervals and frequent measurements. If turbulence is low, use longer intervals and less frequent measurement.

After the radar screens are defined, scan them for crucial information at fixed intervals. And record the information in a structured and accessible format to keep track of how the indicators are changing. Using radar screens contributes to stability by providing the necessary information to assess key developments in the environment, making the stability threats tangible and enabling a search for the right solutions. All the data obtained from the radar screens are put to use in the war room, and that's our next stop.

CHAPTER 27

The war room

Sifting information from different sources

Using the data provided by the radar screens, the staff in the war room tries to find solutions. On the road to Cannes, what if something goes wrong? You have taken a wrong turn and have no clue where you are. You'll try to match the unfamiliar names on road signs with the names on your map. Or you forgot your passport. You might find that a lengthy detour through a deserted border crossing is the quickest way to Cannes. You hear on the radio that an accident has caused a huge traffic jam ahead. You'll consider an alternative route. Or the temperature drops below freezing, transforming the road into an ice skating rink. You may be forced to spend an extra night in a motel.

If even a drive to Cannes is such a potential minefield, what about managing a company in a changing environment? A war room is essential to making the right operational decisions. These will be partly based on your radar screens, but that information is not always sufficient. You might need more focused data, like a weather forecast or a traffic report. You must also draw on your own and your colleagues' experience. That will tell you, for example, not to plan a route through Paris, where you'll surely get bogged down in traffic. Drawing on all its available resources, the war room staff must expose the major problems and make the right operational decisions to keep you on track.

So the war room actually has three information sources (Figure 27.1).

The war room actively collects information from three sources:

- *Radar screens* provide structured and standardized data.
- *Tactics* provide directions through contingency plans, risk analysis, tactical charts, and the stakeholder map.

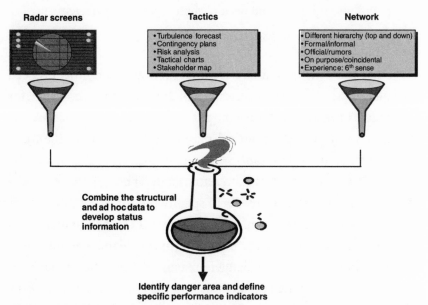

Figure 27.1 The war room first identifies threats based on different sources of information.

- *Network* provides specific, often ad hoc, information. This might include a new organizational structure or environmental information, a customer who is considering a change of direction, or a competitor rolling out a new service, even rumors that might prove important.

All this information needs to be filtered and evaluated. People in the war room have the skill to combine information from these three sources and develop concrete status information for management, helping to identify danger areas and define specific performance indicators. This complex process is but Step 1 in a four-step process:

1. Spot potential danger areas.

2. Perform data analysis in these danger areas to identify critical roadblocks and bottlenecks.

3. Propose solutions and decide whether to alert management.

4. Decide on a response.

Once the danger areas are spotted, the war room must proceed to data analysis, starting by deciding which data to analyze—what, for example, is the actual status compared with the plan, what are the budgets, what does the political map look like, who are the main stakeholders, and what contingency plans have been provided by tactics? Is anything in that data remarkable? Then, drawing on the data analysis, the war room has to specify the threats. To do that, it must know what data are missing and see if it can be obtained. The war room must compare the data with the performance indicators and then narrow down the danger area and the specific bottlenecks. The war room uses the risk analysis and the risk charts provided by Tactics and refines them to narrow down the chance of occurrence, the timing, the critical resources, and the negative impact.

This analysis enables the war room to propose fallbacks and solutions and drives the decision on whether to alert management. It is not always necessary to do so; ringing the alarm bell should be a very selective response. The collective intellect and experience of the war room staff should be drawn on to decide whether to initiate action on its own. Should management be alerted? Would management want the warning or see it as a burden? To decide, the war room needs to weigh management's investment of time against the possible impact of the problem. It's better to sound the alarm once too often than to make a crucial mistake; on the other hand, it's destructive to wear out management with unimportant issues if you wish to maintain credibility. This is a difficult judgment and often involves the corporate culture. Is management paranoid? Then an alarm could create panic and disrupt the whole organization. Does management have the hide of a rhinoceros and need to get poked often to act? If the decision is made to involve management, always propose several solutions and recommend one of them. If the war room is under control, has the necessary information, has performed sound analysis, and is linked to Tactics, it can lead the way with recommendations for decisive concrete action by management.

To decide on the appropriate response in Operations, always take the nature of the threat into account. In general, that corresponds to the 10 identified threats addressed by the radar screen discussed in Chapter 26.

Always consider the impact of the responsive strategy on the objectives and on the main ways to encourage stability. First, consider objectives because changes that have triggered the need for a response can also influence the objectives. A different route to reach the destination may change the objectives. If you execute a response, it can influence the destination and it can influence intermediate objectives. Drawing on collective learning, formulate objectives in more explicit terms as people and stability structures develop over time. Then, consider the impact on the main stability Enablers. You may need to recalculate budgets, reconsider timing agreements and staffing needs, and take account of stakeholders' other interests.

When the response has been decided and mapped out, refine the plans and the organization as needed. Five steps are involved:

1. Appoint people to refine the plan and the organization in close coordination with the war room staff.
2. Agree on the timing of the refined plan and organization.
3. Agree on which external stakeholders to involve.
4. Define up front the criteria for success on which the sign-off of plans and organization will take place.
5. Design a communications plan to launch the changes—an often overlooked consideration.

The war room contributes to stability in several ways. By filtering the critical issues, it greatly reduces the number of possible roadblocks. This allows management to take a focused approach to problem solving. By specializing in problem solving, the war room can reduce the duration of the trouble. The war room continuously creates an overview, which enables a clearer look ahead. It collects and centralizes problems, reducing the distraction of many other people in the organization. And if the war room performs well, management is free to focus on other tasks. That is likely to help management make the right decisions more often.

CHAPTER 28

Adapting to stay on course

Learning to navigate around roadblocks

In spite of your efforts in the war room to anticipate roadblocks, you took a wrong turn. Now you're in Spain. How to proceed? You need to buy a Spanish phrase book. You won't complete the journey as quickly as planned, so you must mollify your family members. You need to find lodging. You must find a new route to Cannes, so you need to study your maps and possibly buy a new one. To prevent a recurrence, perhaps you need more navigational support. Is whoever is sitting next to you in the front the right person or must you draft one of the back-seat passengers?

The "adapt-to-stay-on-course" tool pursues progress by refining plans and the organization to navigate around major roadblocks detected by the war room. Refining plans and refining the organization require four basic steps:

1. Maximize buy-in.
2. Detail the plan.
3. Sell the plan.
4. Implement the plan.

Let's go into these basic steps for refining the plan.

Maximize Buy-In for the Plan. As you are developing tactics to maximize the buy-in, you'll no doubt come across many high-risk areas. It's much to your advantage to avoid them. These might involve *timing*—don't ask for too much work to be done during holidays and don't schedule many important milestones in a very short period of time. Or they might involve human *resources*—ensure that risk areas are not in the hands of inexperienced people, and that many critical resources are not used simultaneously. On the *budget* front, do not draw too heavily on a budget in the beginning and early stages of the change initiative. In the area of *communications,* avoid uncontrolled publicity and clashes with public interest groups and labor unions. Avoid political statements, and avoid tipping your hand to competitors early in the game.

To *plan for early success* involves three main areas: time, human resources, and communications. You want to identify possible and highly visible early successes, go after them, and achieve them. This will strengthen your hand with influential people because it demonstrates your skillfulness, generates enthusiasm, and makes people eager to collaborate with you. You are more likely to achieve this if you commit your best people, your strongest resources, to those early successes. On the communications front, celebrate those successes publicly and with the whole team, so the enthusiasm will become contagious. It's essential to communicate progress and successes to the outside world.

It's also very important to *optimize the environment for your supporters.* Make sure you know who they are, and share your successes with them. In turn, let them communicate their successes themselves. Try to steer your supporters to people who oppose your initiatives—your opponents, in effect. This is the best way to convert opponents because it gives them direct and enthusiastic communications about your successes. Continuously and actively manage the portfolio of your supporters. Maintain awareness within the group, the team, and the organization that supporters need to be kept on your side.

Another important tactic is to *involve stakeholders in the planning process,* and this can be done in three ways. Explain to them up front the value of planning, that is, that the process is essential to ensure you achieve your result. Help them see the value they will derive from your planning effort. Wherever possible, let these people make their own plans—within the boundaries of the overall plan—and let them communicate their plans themselves. And encourage stakeholders to commit explicitly to their plan, their results, and their colleagues.

Detail the Plan. To determine the priority of initiatives, use the inputs from strategy and tactics as well as from the continuous risk-reward analysis of all initiatives.

The next step is to identify external milestones before you create a project schedule. These might include the dates on which legislation takes effect or regulatory changes take hold or the dates on which an implementation begins—such as the introduction of a product. All kinds of external milestones could directly and heavily affect your plan, so beware of them and develop your project schedule around them.

You also need an internal milestone plan to spell out clear and simple steps for everyone involved. Use the external milestones as the starting points and the overall framework. Rephrase external milestones into internal milestones and deliverable requirements. Add the most critical internal milestones, starting with the highest-priority subplans. Aim for about 10 highly visible milestones to facilitate overall program communications. You want clear communications, especially in bigger change initiatives. A limited number of milestones make a big project clearer for everyone from a porter to a project manager. This facilitates communication and allows identification of those points in the project that can be celebrated together.

Use these milestones to create the master plan and detail the activities. These milestones might be either a deliverable or a management decision or sign-off. It's important to list all the major stakeholders who provide input and have concrete activities in the realization of the milestones. Internal stakeholders might be people from the product development department or marketing or production; external stakeholders might be suppliers. From this point, you can clearly state how each stakeholder contributes to reaching each milestone. When dates are attached, you have your master plan.

Sell the Plan. Limit the overall number of milestones in the plan, making clear to everybody in the organization which milestones are fixed and which can be changed, making sure people understand the critical points, locking in the critical points, addressing individual's concerns (see Chapter 7), and empowering people to create ownership.

Implement the Plan. Continuously look forward and backward—forward to major milestones that loom ahead or to resource requirements. Look at risk quotations from risk management, quality quotations from quality assurance, the next deliverables, and team product. Keep a sharp eye on the critical path and its adaptations. Look backward to see what milestones have been reached, what resources spent, what milestones remain unmet. Which activities were delayed? Why? What are the consequences? What is the overall quality of team product and of deliverables?

Refinement of the organization involves similar steps:

1. Maximize the buy-in:
   - Design the organization to meet all critical milestones with short-term successes.
   - Show sufficient attention to the most significant tasks.
   - Involve key players in the organizational design.
   - Try to prevent opponents from having critical roles.
   - Place controversial parts of the plan in task forces to allow for a very quick start.

2. Detail the organizational design:
   - Understand the current organization.
   - Determine how best to achieve the milestones by taking a close look at the new plan.
   - Design an organization that reflects people's Motivators and is consistent with existing Triggers and Enablers.
   - Design an organization that allows for the quickest possible start.
   - Identify the most critical resources and organize the management of them. Take care to find the teaching, training, and coaching resources you will need.

3. Sell the organizational design:

- Discuss the most significant changes in advance, so people won't be surprised in public. Keep communications simple.
- Show how interfaces will be managed, especially the critical ones that have to do with realizing the main milestones.
- Sell the new design to everybody involved, not only to the new people or the converts. This often involves a lot of preparation and anticipation of questions.
- Check to make sure people know their roles.

4. Implement the organizational design:

- Agree upon and communicate a start date.
- Inform the inside and the outside world through a communications plan.
- Provide coaching to help people understand their new roles. Prepare answers for their likely questions.
- Measure the progress of setting up the new organization.
- Celebrate the first success to demonstrate publicly that the design works.

How do these adapt-to-stay-on-course techniques contribute to stability? Involving people who will be affected by the changes removes unnecessary worries. Refining plans and refining the organization help to avoid or overcome major roadblocks. Progress and successes create a cooperative and supportive environment. Clear agreements help the organization avoid conflicts and clarify responsibilities; this makes it less likely that people will be delayed by others. Continuous follow-up on subtasks reduces the pressure on important milestones and deliverables. Early successes greatly enhance confidence, spirit, and performance—not just of the people involved but of those on the outside looking in.

CHAPTER 29

Rapid response capability

An extreme way to reduce turbulence

For this most dramatic of tools, let's return to the road to Cannes. Something dreadful occurs and you cannot deal with it yourself: you are involved in an accident. Your companion hits her head and is bleeding; you're stuck in the wrecked car and can't open the doors. With your mobile phone, you call for help. The police and an ambulance arrive and use their experience and special skills to extract you from the car and rush you to the hospital. Your partner's injury is treated and proves not as serious as it looked. You call your insurer and a replacement car is on its way. The children recover from the shock and are content, for now, to eat ice cream in the cafeteria. By morning, things may be back to normal and you will be able to continue your trip. You realize how fortunate you are that specialized, well-trained teams were available to provide assistance and that you had the right tools—a mobile phone and insurance—in place. In most corporations, no comparable emergency team exists to rescue you from unexpected calamities. So set one up, and make sure it can respond quickly and effectively (Figure 29.1).

The rapid response capability (RRC) has close ties to Tactics and operates in an area that Tactics addresses. Remember the matrix to identify blind spots (Chapter 22). Use this to position the rapid response capability.

The key point of the rapid response capability is that it prepares you for minimizing the impact when something unknown and unexpected occurs (Figure 29.2). Consider this decision.

If something hits you, you need to evaluate it. Was the impact small or large? If small, you don't need the rapid response capability. If it's large, you must decide if the damage creates an urgent problem. If not urgent, you have time to assess the problem and find solutions, so you don't need the rapid response capability. But if the problem is both large

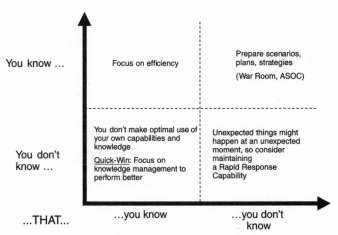

Figure 29.1 A rapid response capability can be an answer to manage unexpected calamities.

and urgent, you should consider the rapid response capability. First, ask yourself if there are other ways to solve this problem. The rapid response capability is an extreme solution and should be used only for urgent problems of large impact that you cannot solve in any other way.

To use this capability, you need to create a network of people who specialize in solving these sorts of problems. The different stability

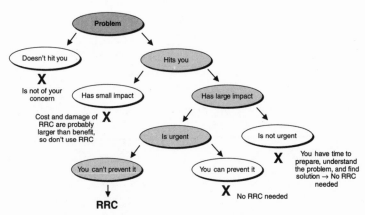

Figure 29.2 The rapid response capability handles only urgent problems that you cannot prevent and that hit with large impact.

structures require different arrangements of this response capability. In unstable environments where many urgent problems arise, you might want the rapid response capability available full time. In environments with fewer problems, you could organize a loose network of experts that could be activated at short notice.

Use of the rapid response capability involves four steps:

1. Make a quick scan of the calamity and decide whether to launch the rapid response capability.
2. Inform the crisis team and decide whether to execute.
3. Go in and resolve the situation quickly!
4. Provide support afterward to help the organization lick its wounds and recover from the intervention.

How does the rapid response capability contribute to stability? It reduces the time of turbulence with its quick response. It reduces the amplitude of turbulence when a calamity occurs. It increases security and confidence during daily operations. And it provides after-care to reduce the inevitable turbulence created by the dramatic intervention.

CHAPTER 30

Matching tools to structures

The tools work differently, depending on where they're used

L et's examine how these various tools are applied in the different stability structures.

In the *Pyramid,* radar screens focus on time, the actual work done, the number of people, stakeholder needs, budgets, procedures, and efficiency. The war room is efficiency driven. The solutions proposed are related mainly to operational threats; the proposed responsive strategies are supported with a lot of concrete evidence. Specialist problem solving helps management to be efficient. Applying the adapt-to-stay-on-course tool helps management define and communicate milestones and objectives very smartly. Responsibilities and authority are clearly assigned and there's a strong focus on the implementation of the plan, rather than on selling it. The rapid response capability's main focus is to reduce the duration of turbulence and allow for smooth operations to resume as quickly as possible. This allows the Pyramid to return to its effective and efficient mode as soon as possible.

In the *Cube,* the application of the tools is different. Radar screens are focused on people and their mental outlook, their change readiness, their scenarios, the communications among them, who the supporters and opponents are, as well as on risks, and, of course, the portfolio. In the war room, the focus is also on people, and outsiders are often used to allow managers to focus on limiting the time of transition. While the war room is focused on reducing roadblocks during transition, the main focus of the adapt-to-stay-on-course tool is selling the plan, with a limited number of overall milestones. It's focused on letting people understand the critical points, so they are empowered during the transition and able to operate independently between a limited number of fixed milestones. The rapid response capability mainly provides after care to reduce the turbulence as soon as the transition is over.

In the *Cylinder,* radar screens focus on synergies, skill profiles, skill development, resource allocation, team performance, progress to plan, and related projects. The war room is applied in a centralized way to collect solutions to problems. The focus is on efficiency, both of the overall movement and the individual cycles. The key issue is learning and the implementation of the learning mechanism—in other words, skills transfer. The adapt-to-stay-on-course tool is focused on detailing the organizational design and plans for setbacks. It develops master plans for overall long-term direction and has internal milestones, in simple communicable steps, for the individual cycles. The rapid response capability increases the security and confidence in each of the cycle operations.

In the *Sphere,* radar screens ensure that budgets, communications, organization, resource planning, skills profiles, and sponsors are closely monitored. This allows the war room to create an overview that looks ahead, using experts. It's always looking for motivational threats, as people play the numbers. The war room lays out and maps responses, partly based on "gut feel," minimizes "wrong routes," and focuses on effectiveness rather than efficiency and political threats. The adapt-to-stay-on-course tool focuses mainly on developing tactics to maximize buy-in to change the plan or the organization design as needed. It allows the Sphere to avoid the high-risk areas, plans for early successes, optimizes support, and involves stakeholders in the planning process. The rapid response capability's focus is to reduce the amplitude or impact of turbulence when a calamity occurs.

In Part 3 we will dive deeper into the art and practice of stabilization, as we look at teamwork, quality, and communications.

AIDE MÉMOIRE

1. Six aspects of any organization—Strategy, Tactics, Operations, Teamwork, Quality, and Communication—are fundamental to stable innovation.

In addition to their normal roles, Strategy, Tactics, and Operations should focus on doing the *right things* to maximize stability. The greatest potential of *Strategy* is to identify potential turbulence by looking beyond your current mental model. *Tactics* ensures that the strategic choices are followed and translated into understandable language for operations, resulting in the most stable passage. *Operations* ensures that routes that maximize stability are followed.

Tools are available for each of these.

2. Among the Strategy tools are
   - A *nightmare competitor* helps to identify your internal weaknesses, by imagining the worst possible competitor and seeing how it attacks your organization.
   - *Role playing* shows various futures that would result from different philosophies of interacting with your competitors, suppliers, and customers.
   - *Game playing* helps you to understand the assumptions you make about the rules of the market. This can provide an understanding of which rules are explicit, which are unwritten, and which can be broken or bent.
   - *Pattern recognition* helps you to understand the trends you are following and allows for learning from other industries that are a step ahead.
   - *Scenario planning* provides you with insight into the uncertainties of the market, helping you to prepare robust strategies for whatever might unfold.

3. In many ways the umbrella of Managing Tactics is a tool in itself. Specific Tactics tools include

STRATEGY enables planning and appropriate timing of periods of calm and transition. TACTICS makes it possible to learn strategic priorities during times of calm and apply this knowledge in making operational choices during times of transition. OPERATIONS gives reliable milestones and tangible deliverables in periods of calm and quickest transition in times of change. TEAMWORK creates a feeling of comfort in which individuals are more willing to take risks and change faster during the transition. QUALITY encourages highest performance during times of consolidation and creates safety nets to let people move more quickly in times of transition. COMMUNICATION stresses continuity despite transitions as well as encourages rapid aligned behavior during transitions.	STRATEGY broadens the portfolio and so increases the odds. TACTICS helps manage the portfolio and so increases the chances of success overall. OPERATIONS creates the conditions to keep as many options open as possible for the lowest investment while maintaining the most stable route forward. TEAMWORK creates a culture in which individuals are encouraged to be entrepreneurial as a result of which the organization can manage all the challenges at the same time. QUALITY creates the conditions to empower people and allows for experimentation. COMMUNICATION speeds the process of letting go of past initiatives and starting new ones by celebrating good failures and sharing the excitement of fresh opportunities.
STRATEGY helps to foresee environmental changes a long way up front enabling incremental innovation. TACTICS provides the perfect bridge between Strategy and Operations to ensure incremental changes. OPERATIONS realizes incremental improvements in the most efficient and effective way. TEAMWORK builds redundancy in the organization so that unusual effects can be handled more smoothly. QUALITY creates an accurate, detailed, and manageable description of current reality. COMMUNICATION reinforces consistency of structure and measures, encourages aligned incremental improvement, and helps prevent transition breaking up into a Lewin change.	STRATEGY opens the eyes of people to see whether a specific flexibility is and will remain relevant. TACTICS ensures that operational learning from the cycle is applied to strategic decisions. OPERATIONS provides detailed planning for each of the individual cycles and steers the overall movement of the whole. TEAMWORK ensures the vital learning capabilities so necessary to make the Cylinder roll smoothly. QUALITY highlights the largest common denominators of disruption and builds them into the organization. COMMUNICATION increases the smoothness within cycles and the transition between cycles by providing access to appropriate know-how and reinforcing continuity.

Tools for Strategy, Tactics, Operations, Teamwork, Quality, and Communication.

- *Structured idea management,* which helps to uncover hidden existing knowledge and facilitate collective new thinking by generating ideas and developing them into an action plan.
- *Risk management* helps to identify the roadblocks, assess their impact, and determine the way around them.
- *Contingency planning* describes, for a specific risk, that you cannot manage the actions that should be taken when the risk occurs.

4. The Operations tools include
   - *Radar screens,* which scan and monitor crucial standardized information, using an intelligence network within the company.
   - The *war room,* which detects potential danger, alerts management to threats, and suggests possible solutions for operations.
   - *Adapting-to-stay-on-course* tactics, which help management to implement and carry out responses by refining plans and organization.
   - *Rapid response capability,* which minimizes turbulence when the unexpected happens and allows management to adapt rigorously.

Part 3

Teams, Quality, and Communication

CHAPTER 31

Collaborating for stability through individualism

Building teams around strong individuals

S port teams that excel and win championships, we all know, require a combination of individual excellence and teamwork. We've all seen groups where however many excellent individuals are on the field at once, the team does not succeed. We've also seen teams with no excellent individuals, which, however hard they work, seldom reach the top levels of competition.

Teams can play a substantial role in creating stability throughout an organization.

In the Pyramid, teamwork ensures minimal disruption because the essence of a team is to build in redundancy. This allows unusual effects to be handled more smoothly than they could be without teams. In the Cube, teamwork minimizes the amount of disruption, by creating a team feeling of comfort, so each individual is willing to take risks and change faster. In the Cylinder, teamwork ensures that vital learning capabilities run smoothly and efficiently. In the Sphere, teamwork creates a culture in which individuals are encouraged to be entrepreneurial, allowing the organization to manage all challenges at the same time.

Let's take a closer look.

In the Pyramid, local disruption can be handled more efficiently with teamwork, which can be a base for incremental improvements: several small steps equal one larger step. Teamwork compensates for the shortcomings of the efficient organization by allowing cross-functional working groups. Teamwork gives people a feeling of membership, which in itself has a damping effect on individual, emotional reactions.

In the Cube, teamwork helps to minimize the period of transition. Teamwork creates the necessary redundancy to deal with the things you don't know that you don't know. Teamwork helps to move individuals; it is much easier to move a team than to move many individuals separately. Teamwork creates a culture of comfort that allows individuals to take risks. And teamwork is a natural way to get all the necessary skills and experiences on board. All these advantages are needed for the difficult and complicated process of the transition through spasmodic innovation.

In the Cylinder, teamwork ensures that learning keeps the Cylinder going. Teamwork creates a home in an always-changing environment. Teamwork is the only effective base from which experts can work together on several tasks simultaneously, leveraging their resources. Teamwork creates an optimal environment for people to share learning.

In the Sphere, teamwork is a core competence of the operation as a whole. Teamwork holds the enterprise together by providing the base from which individual expertise can be used in different places at the same time. Teamwork increases individuals' chances of success and creates the culture necessary to allow individuals and teams to manage the risks and to follow up on many opportunities.

That teams are so important hardly diminishes the role of the individual. The best teamwork is based on the individualism of its members. In a world where individuals have more and more freedom and flexibility in choosing their work, where lifelong employment is unusual and demand for high-caliber people exceeds the supply, people can make choices, and they do. They change jobs and go where they want to go. At the same time, companies face increasingly complex challenges for which they need and want high-caliber personnel. Indeed, companies are coming to understand that the only truly scarce resource is people. This leads to a situation in which individual needs and wants are becoming pivotal in establishing and running teams within companies. Creating teams based on the individuals, or what we call *I-teams*, helps companies to tackle the challenges that cause this disruption.

How do we define an I-team? Like any team, it's a (small) number of people with a common purpose, producing common products, judged by a set of performance goals, with a common approach to which they hold themselves accountable. However, the I-team puts special emphasis on the additional principle that the *individual* adds value to and gains value from the team. We'd like to discuss I-team principles and tools, how to use the tools, and how the tools can be applied in different structures.

What are the basic principles and tools for an I-team?

1. Focus on the "I," getting the best out of individuals. The tool is *The SWIP Mirror.*

2. Create an environment in which individuals are encouraged to form and work together in I-teams, based on optimizing the *adding value to* and *gaining value from* principle. The tool is *Manage the Marketplace.*

3. Create a natural balance for individuals, teams, and the organization by insisting on balanced structure and timing of events. The tool is *Balance the Biorhythms.*

We'll focus on them in the next few chapters.

CHAPTER 32

Mirror, mirror

A tool for self-assessment and for weighing colleagues

The SWIP Mirror is a tool that helps individuals plan their futures and, at the same time, helps teams to plan for their individuals. Individuals look at the Mirror to get an idea of their own Strengths, Weaknesses, Interest, and Potential (SWIP). At the same time, team members look at the individuals—and at how the individuals look at themselves. The result of all this is that the individuals work out a plan for themselves, while the team can make a plan for the role of the individual in the team. The benefits are that you usually wind up with self-confident individuals who can see their paths to the future and you create an environment in which a team has the right expectation for the individual and can help the individual stay on the path.

The SWIP Mirror process consists of four phases:

1. During the first phase, the individual is asked to make an initial strengths and weaknesses profile and to take stock for the first time of personal interests. The output is a very personal profile of Strengths, Weaknesses, and Interest.

2. During the second phase, the individual is compared with peers, allowing for a benchmark of individual strengths and weaknesses—a calibrated profile.

3. During the third phase, the individuals are asked to play back their history, with the aim of understanding why certain key choices were made. In this way they can create a SWIP profile.

4. In the fourth phase, the individuals prepare an action plan, in order to be better prepared for the key decisions that they are going to make in the near term.

Holding up the SWIP Mirror helps teams and individuals to achieve stability. The individuals find out what they really want.

So they know what they want in a team. The team can tell the individuals what they can get out of the team. In parallel, teams can express their needs while the individuals can explain how they can help fulfill them. SWIP helps the individuals to understand their strengths, helping them to base a future on their potential differentiating factors. On the flip side, sharing one's weaknesses allows others to consider them and to present potential improvement points. Understanding one's interests (resulting from one's values, aspirations, and constraints) gives both the individuals and the team the opportunity to understand the individuals' motivation. Exploiting one's potential helps individuals to better prepare to choose among the wide variety of opportunities offered in the future.

SWIP is also crucial for creating balanced, effective, and personally rewarding teams. It helps individuals to select the teams in which they can make an optimal contribution and grow. It helps team members identify gaps in the team lineup, influencing future choices. It helps team members to be open and to understand each other, creating respect and tolerance. For both the team and the individuals, SWIP helps to create a language for exchanging constructive feedback, helping one another grow.

Let's go through the SWIP process from the perspective of two team members.

The first is a young, ambitious, and so far very successful "eager beaver." SWIP challenged her ability to accept outside criticism. During the first phase, she found many strengths, limited weaknesses, and tremendously broad interest. The outcome was that she felt absolutely self-confident (young, successful, and ambitious people almost always feel this way). In fact, during this first phase, anyone is likely to create an extremely unbalanced profile.

In the second phase, it emerged that not all her strengths were really key. Relative weaknesses emerged. Most often people will discover, in this second phase, more about what is really important to them. This step represents a delicate moment because you don't want an individual to become shaky, but instead to become puzzled and open to new thoughts.

During the third phase, the eager beaver asked herself, "Why did I choose this job?" and "Why did I go to a university, anyway?" This helped her understand what her drivers were. At the end of this phase she understood her capabilities and ambitions. People tend to feel that going through this phase of the process helps them better understand their ambitions, values, and constraints.

In general, a young and ambitious person needs relatively little time to go through a SWIP process, but several SWIPs are needed to make a plan of action.

Let's go through the process again, this time with a 50-year-old middle manager in midlife crisis.

In the first phase, you discover that he doesn't feel he has many strengths. He talks about his weaknesses, things that have gone wrong, things he is bad at. Discussions of interest are narrowly focused and of limited interest. He is not confident about the future, asking himself, "What did I do with my life?"

During the second phase you can help him uncover strengths he has forgotten. You can help him focus on and note his weaknesses— but encourage him not to overreact to them. You can help him exploit some interests and build self-esteem.

In the third phase you uncover potential future building blocks. You help him to know potential pitfalls; you can help him clarify his interests. Most often, at this point, the individual will have a balanced look at himself.

In the final phase, he knows what to avoid; he knows his weaknesses inside out. Often he knows what to invest in, and wants to build upon for the future. He also has a clear view on when he will be happy.

In general, an individual like this needs a lot of time to go through a SWIP process—a couple of meetings, a couple of sessions, and a couple of weeks of throughput time. In the end, though, he'll be able to develop a plan much faster than the younger person. For the team the enormous advantage is that you can add a very experienced, very knowledgeable person with enormous drive.

CHAPTER 33

Managing the marketplace

Optimizing supply and demand among personnel

The second I-team tool is *Managing the Marketplace.* This tool helps to create an environment in which individuals can find and perform in I-teams, based on *adding value to* and *gaining value from* the team. Each stability structure has its own type of market and its own mechanisms, so you should ensure that the people within each stability structure have access to the appropriate marketplaces.

Marketplace mechanisms optimize supply and demand, creating freedom for the individual to maximize the I-team principles of *adding value to* and *gaining value from* a team. Marketplace mechanisms give individuals the freedom to find their preferred work, so they can develop in the direction they choose. This maximizes *gaining value from* a team. So clearly, individuals' motivations are a key to achieving great results. When there is complete openness and free flow of market information, individuals will try to add value in the best way they can, creating better results and maximizing the added value to a team. Because scarcity is rewarded, people will automatically develop and market scarce skills. Performing well leads to more freedom in choosing work in the marketplace.

How best to describe the marketplace, a place where supply and demand meet and try to come to a settlement? We have found seven different elements in this environment:

1. What are the rules of the market? Is the market open and fair?

2. Who is the regulator? Who ensures that the market follows the rules?

3. What is the rhythm of the marketplace? What is the fluctuation of supply and demand—do people think about taking a job for years or taking on a task for weeks or months?

4. What is the task, the challenge, the future job to be fulfilled? These are the keys to the supply side of the market.

5. What is the major currency for trading (skills, personality, experience)? This is the key to the demand side.

6. What is the leadership? Who are the trend setters, the market makers whom everybody watches to determine the mood of the market?

7. Is there freedom to "not buy"? How free is the individual to say "no"?

As we've noted, each different structure needs a different marketplace.

In the Pyramid, the marketplace is like a centralized economy. In the Cube, the marketplace is like an auction house. At a certain moment, after a long period of preparation during which goods are acquired and customers cultivated, the marketplace is full of desirable goods and bidders who want them. To be successful, the auction house must be prepared, with a team that has all the necessary skills to: understand the area of expertise and the real value of something, as well as the ability to find the right customers. In the Cylinder, the marketplace is somewhat like itinerant musicians. Many jazz musicians travel the world, playing where they find work, from cafés to jazz festivals. Some performances are scheduled, especially for established acts, but many are spontaneous. Musicians form combos based on who is around and what they feel like playing. Often what motivates them is what will be the most fun. In the Sphere, the marketplace is like a big-city real estate market. You often have little time to think: Act quickly before the opportunity is lost. You don't have time to get all the capabilities on board that you wish you had. Act now or the chance to act may vanish.

Let's look at each of these in turn.

In the centrally regulated economy of the Pyramid, regulation and information flow are high. Everybody knows what the job offers are, everybody knows what the career ladders are, and everybody knows what everybody else is doing. The key regulator is the central staff in the head office's personnel department. The marketplace rhythm is measured in years. The most important information is about the type of issue you'll need to address, the type of job you're going to fill, and the risks that need to be managed when taking the job. In a Pyramid, it can take at least three successes to make up for one failure, so failures are to be avoided. The major currency for trading is what you bring to the job: skill, power, political connections. The leadership and the market makers are always drawn from the top of the hierarchy. These people set the trends and decide what the future looks like. The ability to say "no" to a next job is very limited.

In the Cube's auction-house environment, regulation and information flow are high during the periods of relative calm. But during the transition phases, the flow of accurate and up-to-date information is low—nobody knows exactly what is happening. The regulator is the centralized strategic staff. The marketplace rhythm is inconsistent. In relative calm, people think in terms of years, but in times of change, the rhythm is weak and can be hard to find. The most important information about jobs is the urgency of getting the job done and the skills needed. The major currency for taking a job is having the skills required during transition. The trend setters and market makers are based on situation, reputation, and personality. The ability to "not buy" is available only when somebody else comes forward who is more capable.

In the Cylinder's world of roaming musicians, regulation is medium and information flow is low. The regulator is an informal network of people who know each other. The rhythm is measured in weeks and months. The most important information is about starting time and duration of the job and the necessary experience. The leadership and the trend setters are based on initiative and acceptance. The major currency for trading and getting a job is experience and reputation. The ability to say "no" to a job is very high: Nobody forces you to do something you don't want to.

In the Sphere's urban real estate market, regulation and information flow are nonexistent. The rhythm is in hours, at most days. The most important information is about issues, tasks, challenges, and future jobs: What are the content and the context? Who is on the team? What is the chance of winning? The major currency is your informal network, your personality, your way of thinking—and your reputation for being a winner. Leadership and the trend setters are based on initiative and acceptance. The ability to "not buy" is very high.

CHAPTER 34

I got rhythm

Body clock or calendar,

natural rhythms enhance stability

The third I-team tool is *Balancing Biorhythms.* This puts in place the natural pulse necessary for creating stability in teams. Biorhythms function as a constant stability factor, even in times of disruption. Biorhythms are a natural phenomenon (day-night, weeks, months, individuals' bodies, mental and emotional rhythms). Biorhythms enhance the flow within teams and optimize the use of energy. Teams can more quickly go through the different stages of Forming, Storming, Norming, and Performing (the model proposed by the psychologist B.W. Tuckman in 1965) by using the right biorhythms.

In the Pyramid, the key Biorhythm principle ensures the consistency of performance. In the Cube, it ensures that high team performance coincides with the transition. In the Cylinder, you have to ensure that the rhythm reflects the learning. In the Sphere, you have to ensure that Biorhythm principles create a home feeling.

In a Pyramid, team Biorhythms are implemented through regular planning and progress meetings. The steady Biorhythm helps members stay focused on the mission instead of attending only to day-to-day priorities. This is essential particularly when team members are not working full time on the job. Regular meetings allow individuals to depend on them. Regularity in the meetings also ensures that risks are not forgotten in the day-to-day operations. A team can be successful in the Pyramid only if its Biorhythm is in sync with the powerful Biorhythms of the rest of the Pyramid organizations, including communication events, budget cycles, production cycles, and yearly plans. All these are based on biorhythms within the Pyramid.

In a Cube, Biorhythms help to maintain preparedness for the crucial moment to come. When you refer, for example, to the Tuckman model of Forming, Storming, Norming, and Performing, it is essential to remember that, for a Cube, timing is crucial. During relative calm, you train your teams and ensure they have reached the Performing stage in time for the transition.

Biorhythms in the Cylinder help to enhance the learning by adapting the rhythm of the Cylinder and of the teams to the natural learning cycle. Take David Kolb's learning cycle, for example. Kolb postulated a continuous cycle of Doing, Reflecting, Connecting, and Deciding. Since learning is the key to creating stability, Biorhythms in sync with the natural learning cycle help teams to learn better and more quickly. Most organizations do not take enough time for reflection; it is too often perceived as "doing nothing," rather then stepping back and looking at what you did. Reflection is a critical step in the learning cycle, and regularly scheduled reflection sessions help teams to make reflection a natural part of doing business. That enhances the company's ability to learn.

In a Sphere, Biorhythms create stability by making sure there is a regular pattern in the timing of events, creating that necessary "home feeling." Best-in-class Spheres find natural ways for members to meet each other; one is to introduce a Biorhythm around heritage and tradition (such as formal dinners or award ceremonies).

These tools are applied differently in the different structures, and we'll examine that in the next chapter.

CHAPTER 35

Matching teams' tools to structures

How operational tools fit the different structures

Let's look at how the tools are applied in the different stability structures.

In the Pyramid. The SWIP Mirror is applied to make explicit the strengths and weaknesses of the individuals of the team. This ensures that no unnecessary risks are taken because of a lack of skills.

Marketplace Mechanisms are used to create a formal marketplace through yearly reviews. They continuously communicate the importance of incremental improvements and the role teams play in this. They ensure that individuals who do not feel at home in a Pyramid can transfer to different places inside or outside the company.

Biorhythms are used to adapt the teams to the organizational rhythms as much as possible through such events as business planning cycles, quarterly results, and yearly reviews. This ensures minimal disruption.

In the Cube. During relative calm, the SWIP Mirror is important to investigate individuals' strengths, weaknesses, interests, and potential. That way, in time of disruption the Cube can count on the right mix of strengths and interests. If talent is scarce, as is often the case, team-building centered on key interests is important to get the team going.

Marketplace Mechanisms are needed to get "aces in their places" in times of transition.

In times of relative calm, focus on hard-line Biorhythms such as training and preparation for action on monthly communication events. In times of transition, Biorhythm is best set by daily communication meetings and for "out-of-the-office" get-togethers to release tensions.

In the Cylinder. SWIP can help you build the necessary expertise by capitalizing on peoples' strengths and interests.

Marketplace Mechanisms are used to provide a smooth transfer of individuals from one cycle to the other.

Biorhythms are used to implement the necessary learning by adhering to Kolb's learning cycle such as organizing regular reflection meetings. To maximize personnel development and learning, plan individual review sessions every 6 months. In these sessions, identify personal goals and evaluate whether they were met.

In the Sphere. Playing the numbers games requires the organization to have the attitude that each individual should be an entrepreneur and that the organization can maximize each individual's potential.

Because most people working here will be entrepreneurial in the first place, setting up a marketplace is not the most important thing; it will arise naturally. Realize that individuals who found and built an opportunity are seldom the best ones to organize it as it grows. Make sure you have enough people within the marketplace to help the others become successful: It is absolutely essential to ensure that teamwork is not constricted by procedures. Remove the power chains, so that the key criterion in the marketplace is the personality of individuals.

Where the business opportunities are all over the place, Biorhythms can help hold the whole together. Regular planning sessions and informal but regular get-togethers can keep everybody up to date. Major investments should be made in annual events that brand the company as a whole.

Beyond teamwork, a commitment to quality and strong quality assurance programs are essential for stability. We'll examine them in the next few chapters.

....

CHAPTER 36

Ensuring performance by allowing mistakes

How Quality Assurance facilitates cross-fertilization—and stability

Quality Assurance (QA) is a prerequisite for maximizing stability. In the next few chapters we'll examine how the quality stabilizer can contribute to stability, what QA tools are available, and how to build them.

In today's turbulent environment, the traditional approach to QA has failed. In visits to companies in recent months, we've heard, "Quality circles have been set up all over my company but learning between circles has not been achieved." In this case, QA was implemented fragmentally. "It was a great effort to receive our ISO quality certificate, but now we're certified, the implementation team is dissembled, and people are falling back into old routines." In this case, quality was treated as a one-time project rather than a continuing process. "Our quality department checks output to specifications. Nowadays they really have problems because specifications are not there or change rapidly." At this company, QA was perceived and treated as a mechanistic process rather than a continuing commitment. "Quality-minded people are the worst. They're obsessed by procedures and signatures and are inflexible in coping with the uncertainty of change." Here, quality has become a harness rather than an inspiration and a source of pride.

So rather than the traditional approach to quality, you need to think of QA as a stabilizer, one that provides guidance on achieving goals and preempts surprises. QA facilitates cross-fertilization of ideas, and it spots gaps and overlaps in activities.

In the *Pyramid*, QA enhances stability by creating an accurate, detailed, and manageable description of the current reality. QA codifies processes. It allows a focus on long-term stability, especially when ISO-certified quality procedures are rigidly embedded in the company's processes. QA allows for planned incremental changes because initial stages are well defined. It aligns functions and responsibilities and empowers people within roles. It creates a focus on doing and delivery, which facilitates learning about content and process. QA helps planners avoid mistakes, ensuring you don't hit hidden problems with your main processes. Finally, it allows for accurate training of people around procedure descriptions and roles, and it enables the design of simulations and safe-failing places.

In the *Cube*, the focus is different. QA allows for the highest possible performance during times of consolidation and creates safety nets to let people move more quickly in times of transition. QA creates an atmosphere for continuous change-readiness, by allowing for Pyramidal performance in delivery and by balancing "doing next" with planning during periods of consolidation. It facilitates quick start-up of the transition and allows for monitoring of the transition. It prevents implementation of overly rigid and otherwise counterproductive procedures. It brings stability because it lets you learn how to perform transitions better and creates safety nets to let people move quickly. QA compensates for the imperfections of teams, and embedded quality allows for a high level of empowerment during transition. Finally, it provides the means to spot and react to mistakes in timely fashion.

In the *Cylinder*, QA minimizes disruption by understanding the broadest common denominators of disruption and embedding that understanding in the organization. It allows for learning about content and for training of experts, ensuring that two sets of measurements become available: within one cycle for short-term measures and over multiple cycles for long-term measures. It creates a focus on maintaining measurements for the next cycle as much as possible. QA finds and designs the balance—an optimal way of working for the whole and firefighting when turbulence comes too fast. Besides this, it provides a mechanism to learn and to improve from feedback. QA takes care of pattern recognition, making the largest common denominators of disruption known and enabling the construction of responses within the organization.

In the *Sphere*, QA reduces disruption by creating the conditions to empower people and allow for experimentation. It prevents people from repeating major mistakes yet encourages them to experiment. It creates safety nets. It facilitates cross-fertilization between each smaller group that "plays the numbers." It provides both feedback and "feed-forward" mechanisms. QA also creates heuristic learning and organizational tolerance for imperfect data. It supports preparation rather than planning. Indeed, it limits the planning by asserting, "Let's do it and learn!" QA continuously develops measures, implements measuring, and measures incessantly to demonstrate achievement of objectives and provide proof of progress. QA also makes sure that "smart mistakes" are rewarded.

The common denominator of all QA tools is that they prevent things from going wrong and prepare contingencies should things go wrong. We'll focus on three tools:

1. *Canaries* provide an early-warning system to reduce troubleshooting and improve performance.

2. *Prototyping the Environment* allows for acceleration of learning in a safe way.

3. *Master-Apprentice Relations* minimize disruption by creating learning relationships that boost effectiveness and efficiency.

Let's now examine each of these tools in depth to see how they can help you use QA to create stability.

CHAPTER 37

Tweet, tweet

An early-warning system
that recognizes disruption

For many decades, canaries were used in coal mines as early-warning tools. Canaries sense a lack of oxygen earlier than people do, and when they do, they start singing loudly. As soon as this alarm sounded, torches were extinguished and people left the mine shaft.

Our "canaries" play the same role. A global telecommunications operator used IT canaries to detect bugs in a new billing system before converting to it—and saved millions of dollars in revenue losses and possible lawsuits from customers. These canaries were senior experts on databases, project management, customer management, and so on. They "flew" around and investigated areas where quality was suspect. They were free to go where they wanted and had no specified deliverables. Rather, they were the eyes and ears of the management and prevented the project from being delayed and having to make costly fixes. Their successful mission prevented people from becoming demoralized and losing motivation.

How do you find or create canaries? First, look for people with a track record of wisdom and experience that makes them sensitive to any "lack of oxygen." Then educate them on what needs to be achieved, so they know the objectives and targets of management and the people in the organization. They need to know, as precisely as possible, where the organization is headed. Empower them to fly about freely, identifying the most critical "branches" to sit on. Failure to empower them and to make sure they have sufficient status to be heard prevents them from adding any value. Use the canaries to alleviate stress and provide a feeling of security. Management should guide them to places where quality is suspect and encourage them to report on what they find and how it compares to the plan.

Allowed to do their job, canaries contribute to stability in several ways. As they fly around, they can coach the coaches. They get to see many areas of the company and their broad focus can unearth important information. Canaries keep people focused and alert, which contributes to stability, and they recognize individual contributions and create the conditions to empower people. Canaries see potential danger early on and prevent people from making major mistakes. They have the skills to develop measurements that can track progress to plan, and they can help design the most stable route forward. Canaries keep risk at acceptable levels and provide a safety net. They also act as a buffer against imperfect data and against the outside world.

CHAPTER 38

Prototypes

Creating safe places to fail

A Japanese car manufacturer has prototyped critical sections of its car-manufacturing process to train its operators, which has helped to produce significant progress in the company's zero-defects program. In this "safe failing space," new operators are trained and certified; those with a record of serious mistakes are retrained. High operator involvement is required, and the impact of operator mistakes is high. Trial production of new models takes place partly in this environment to fine-tune production technology.

Probably the best-known example of the prototyping tool is the flight simulator, used widely to train pilots for both civil and military aviation. Pilots can be forced to go beyond their limits in flight simulators—and thus learn what their limits are. This safe failing space allows pilots to master many situations and to tap into the worldwide collective learning integrated into global training programs.

How do you build this tool? It's a four-step process:

1. Create a prototype. Research the available technologies and the environment in which the prototype has to work. Research the people who will use the prototype, including the instructors and trainees. Form hypotheses and make assumptions about what kind of problems need to be simulated. Draw up a list of specifications for the prototype and for its environment. These specifications have to be linked, just as the prototype and the environment are linked. Use the specifications to design, develop, and produce the prototype.

2. Use the prototype to train people and accelerate their learning. Make certain that skills learned in the prototype are transferred outside the prototype.

3. Evaluate the prototype frequently and on a regular basis. Collect feedback from participants; define the lessons learned, asking both

the students and the instructors. Suggest prototype improvements and specify those improvements.

4. Refine the prototype. Consider all possible sources for ideas, including management, legislation, competition, customer needs, accident reports, and the current prototype. If you imbed this entire cycle into your organization, you can build a future-proof prototype that will implement and test whatever refinements are recommended. Short-circuiting the refinement process can lead to reliance on a bad prototype, which can create the opposite effect from what you hoped for.

In applying the prototyping tool, always make sure that you maximize the learning opportunity. Be creative. Train the instructors to guide and coach learning inside the prototype. Never punish people for making sensible mistakes. The whole idea behind this prototyping tool is to push people to their limits, and beyond—to force them to make mistakes, so they learn from them (you should consider *rewarding* people for sensible mistakes). We strongly recommend that this tool be used to simulate only anticipated problems, rather than forcing people to deal with issues or problems they will not be working with—as if the Japanese car manufacturer were to confront people on the production end with problems originating in purchasing. Everyone involved in the process should focus on transferring the skills learned on the prototype to the real world outside.

Prototyping the environment brings stability in several ways. It can be used to select, assess, and test the best people and to train them to the highest possible level of performance. Trainers can provide leadership when the unexpected erupts. Lessons learned in real life can be studied in simulation exercises and can be used to translate processes, systems, and procedures. Prototyping the environment protects core processes by creating safe failing spaces. The transfer of knowledge and skills is maximized, as responses to all anticipated problems can be prepared in a relatively short time. Prototyping the

environment allows for testing and refinement of roles and procedures, as well as for simulation of plans. It allows for mass certification
relatively quickly and at the lowest cost. It allows for empowerment in
times of calm and of turbulence. Responses to new and unexpected
turbulence can be developed quickly. Prototyping the environment
can also be used to define and test improvements, and it can help
determine which parts of an organization are most likely to be
affected by the turbulence and how they will be affected.

CHAPTER 39

"Yes, Master"

One measure of experts is how well they pass on knowledge

R embrandt van Rijn was a genius not just at painting but also at increasing the output of his studio by using apprentices. Demand for his paintings was high, so Rembrandt used several apprentices at the same time, teaching them to emulate his technique, composition, and the use and mixing of colors. As a result, the volume of the output of his studio improved significantly, which allowed for high responsiveness while maintaining high quality.

At first glance you might think Rembrandt and Taco Bell, a fast-food chain in the United States, have little in common. But Taco Bell also makes good use of the master-apprentice tool. Employees are hired for their attitude and then trained for competence by senior, experienced employees. They learn multiple tasks as they rotate through several jobs. At peak times, when large lines form at the counter, any employee can call out "Aces in their places." Immediately all the employees move to do the job they're most familiar with. The result is that Taco Bell gets top ratings on customer service and also on being a good company to work for.

How do you create master-apprentice relationships? First, find masters capable of guiding and teaching apprentices. Rembrandt, for example, even employed other masters who worked with the apprentices. Leverage the experience by creating mechanisms that encourage asking for and providing help. This will create an environment where not only masters provide assistance but where people get comfortable helping each other and accepting shared responsibility for standards.

Master-apprentice relationships need not migrate into boss-employee relationships, although they sometimes do. In selecting a master, the dominant criterion is not who sits where in the hierarchy but who can best provide expert coaching on both process and content. In some complex situations, multiple masters might be used, but in these cases the responsibilities and the authority of each need to be defined very precisely to avoid conflict.

Master-apprentice relationships create stability by providing instant feedback on problems of content and process. They help people through the first uncertain period of a new job. They prepare people, support them, and empower them. They limit the planning that people engage in, which is useful because people new in their jobs often place a heavy emphasis on planning. Masters stimulate people to get into the doing as soon as possible and to learn while doing. Masters keep their apprentices inspired. They make sure sensible mistakes are rewarded. They teach the apprentices how to avoid sources of disruption and how to cope with them. From a cultural perspective, masters create stability because they reinforce the strength of a company. They teach the apprentices to work according to the agreed forms and they keep them focused. They are responsible for the quality of the apprentices and, as part of that, they stimulate the apprentices' quality awareness. Masters also transfer the culture and the informal rules that are the glue of many organizations. They allow people to adapt to a new situation gradually and serve as a buffer until they do. And the presence of apprentices forces masters to make as explicit as possible the implicit knowledge they have. This maintains and improves the masters' own skills and expertise.

In the end, masters also encourage apprentices to leverage their learning among others. And master-apprentice relationships endure, often deepening over time. This can prove a great source of strength and stability to a company.

CHAPTER 40

Matching tools to toolboxes

Each quality tool works differently
in the different structures

Each of these tools is built and applied differently in each stability structure.

In the *Pyramid,* canaries are used infrequently, and, if used, are allocated to planning. The prototyping-the-environment tool is used mainly to realize incremental improvement, which can be planned for and trained upon in "safe failing spaces." It is also used to test skills and procedures before transferring people outside the prototype. Master-apprentice relationships are an important vehicle to let Pyramids gradually and slowly improve, by focusing on doing and delivery. They facilitate learning on both the content and the process. Rules, procedures, and policies need to be explained and trained. In a Pyramid, the master-apprentice relationship can migrate into a boss-employee relationship. Experienced masters in a Pyramid serve as a buffer to the outside world.

In the *Cube,* canaries act as safety nets and are created to let people move more quickly in times of transition. Canaries suggest changes and cluster them in short, effective bursts. They play an important role in suggesting the right moment and the best way to execute the transition phase. In that way they also act as buffers against disruptions. Their presence prevents other people from being distracted. Canaries are the most important means in a Cube to monitor the transition, as they can go everywhere. Prototyping the environment is mainly used as preparation for empowerment; it allows the highest level of empowerment possible during the transition. It can also be used to train for transition effectiveness.

In the *Cylinder,* canaries are used to understand the common denominators and to help design plans to handle multiple changes. Canaries serve as coaches for the masters and make certain that overall movement goes into the right direction. Masters train people on both process and content.

In the *Sphere,* master-apprentice relationships help people to be productive in an environment where many options have to be kept open. They help people with planning that is based on results, avoiding a focus on the steps to get there: They help people *do* instead of *plan.*

Communication, too, can be a powerful tool for stability, provided it is tuned to the specific requirements of the different stability structures. We'll take a look at how that can be done in the next few chapters.

CHAPTER 41

Applying the power of the word

Communication tools foster understanding of how stability structures work

C ommunication helps align behavior during turbulence and increases the responsiveness of your organization and its people by helping them quickly understand what is going on. Communication is a *key* element in explaining the stability structures, fostering understanding of their appropriateness and how they work. In this chapter we'll examine the communication tools available for increasing stability and the differences to keep in mind when applying them in the different structures.

In the *Pyramid,* communication reinforces the consistency of the structure and its measures, and it encourages aligned incremental improvement. It helps to prevent incremental creep from breaking up into a Lewin change. Communication must be clear and must prevent overload for people in the organization. In the *Cube,* communication has a double role. It must focus on stable issues like vision and common goals. It also has to encourage initiative and creativity during periods of transition. In the *Cylinder,* communication increases the smoothness within the cycles and the smoothness of the surge between the cycles. It does this by providing access to the appropriate know-how and by reinforcing continuity, often through information systems. In the *Sphere,* communication speeds the process of letting go of past initiatives and starting new ones—by celebrating both the good and the "good failures." Communication is often ad hoc because of the unpredictability and high frequency of events. This requires flexible communication tools. Communication also helps to spread the excitement of fresh opportunities.

Sharing the knowledge of lessons learned from previous experiences with turbulence is important to maximize stability. The knowledge can differ with each stability structure. In the *Pyramid,* the most important element that everybody has access to is the lessons learned in previous incremental improvement projects (actions taken, people involved, results achieved) within the organization. That way they don't have to reinvent the wheel: They can simply say, "A ha! That's what we did last time!" They'll know what steps to take, and that makes the process much easier and smoother for all involved. In the *Cube*, people involved need an outline of the previous transition process as well as typical time schedules for transitions. In the *Cylinder*, make sure that people are aware of the best-practice processes for their cycle. This will incorporate knowledge of the improvements from the previous cycle. In the *Sphere*, everyone must have knowledge of two elements: What can I do with initiatives to make the hit rate as high as possible? What can I learn from past field experiences or field initiatives about why an idea was successful or unsuccessful?

Organizational culture is an important component of sharing lessons learned. Try to build a culture of openness. Make sure everybody provides information in a constructive way. Make sure everybody is taken seriously and listened to carefully. Make sure everybody feels the environment is safe for sharing information. Create a culture of giving as well as receiving. Make sure you don't fall into the pitfalls that face each of the structures.

In the *Pyramid*, the mental model might exist that there is no need to share knowledge "because everything is known within the organization." People don't take the time to share information with each other because efficiency is so important. The solution is to make sharing lessons learned a criterion that is mentioned prominently in each person's evaluation. In the *Cube*, the culture might bring with it a strong "not invented here" attitude about all new information. As a result, people don't know what information is important to them. The solution is to make sure that recognized "heroes" engage in information sharing. That process will create a willingness to absorb information. In the *Cylinder*, expertise is highly valued and because knowledge could be seen as a source of power, people may be unwilling to share what they know. One solution is to do what BASF did: redefine the role of the expert from someone who *has* knowledge to someone who *shares* knowledge with those who need it. In the *Sphere,* too, "not invented here" may be a problem. The fast flow of information makes it difficult for people to understand what is important for others. The intuition of star people is the best filtering mechanism that you can get in this overflow of information.

In the next chapters, we will show how two classic forms of business communications differ for each of the stability structures:

Tailored Communication, which provides people with information relevant to their positions. Information can be tailored by position in the organization and by the occurrence of turbulence or an event. This targeting can prevent information overload. It also helps align individuals' behavior as they deal with turbulence and go through innovation, reassuring them that their Enablers and Triggers will remain stable.

Crisis Communication reduces disruption by informing people quickly about what's going on. This dampens uncertainty and increases people's responsiveness to crises.

CHAPTER 42

If the suit fits . . .

Knowing whom to contact and when makes

for effective communicating

The first aspect of communication we will cover is *Tailored Communication*. Some messages are *segment*-specific while others are driven by *timing*. Tailored Communication involves consideration of the characteristics, the driving force, and the restraining forces for each segment you are trying to reach. Let's assume the segments are

- Sponsors, including the CEO and some board members
- Facilitators, including labor unions and bosses
- Doers, the people most directly involved
- Supporters

Sponsors are available when "big guns" are needed, but basically their limited role is to bless (and perhaps kick off) the proceedings. Facilitators are of two distinct types—the workers' unions and the workers' bosses. Facilitators make resources available, often people and sometimes financial, and they need to be sufficiently involved so they remain comfortable providing these resources. When facilitators start to become uncomfortable, they can turn into Disablers and start blocking initiatives. Doers are those most directly involved: they do the work. Involving them makes them agents of change rather than its victims. The last group, Supporters, is somewhat peripheral. Supporters are people you need to involve in some way to help you achieve your change but who themselves will not be directly affected. You might want people from the finance department to record an additional line of information on the monthly business reports, for example. You need their involvement, but they aren't directly affected by your change initiative.

Let's consider the most effective way to communicate with each group.

The Sponsors. Sponsors mainly focus on performance, so they want to understand the financial figures and the results. They don't want to be swamped by detail; they have many other concerns. Their driving force, generally, is improving the company in the long term. The restraining force is that the consequences of innovations are unclear to them. So the tailored information they need is financial results and what action is being taken to knock down any barriers that arise.

How do you deal with the Sponsors within each stability structure? In the *Pyramid,* stress that building stability by innovating maximizes long-term financial results. Make sure they communicate to the rest of the organization the urgency of handling the turbulence *now,* so it does not become disruptive along the incremental path. In the *Cube,* Sponsors need to understand that financial results must be averaged over periods of calm and of transition—the long term. A short-term view would lead them to conclude that transition is bad for the company. In the *Cylinder,* Sponsors need to know how the cycles themselves are being improved to show them how capturing knowledge in each cycle will improve financial results over the long run. In the *Sphere,* Sponsors need to understand that working on many initiatives simultaneously is the only way to ensure having at least one winner. This means they must also understand that having many failures is not bad, so long as they are accompanied by successes. They have to accept that going in different directions at the same time helps to realize their vision for the company and ensures the best long-term performance.

The Facilitators. Let's start with the unions. They are most interested in collective agreements and social issues. Driving forces are usually an improvement of working conditions and achieving gains in the collective bargaining agreement because those are the issues by which the people they represent evaluate them. A restraining force is their fear that innovation and change will translate into downsizing or that working conditions will deteriorate. They need to receive guarantees about working conditions and the social effects on employees.

The message should be, "Your company really cares for the employees and shows this by handling turbulence so its impact is minimized."

In the *Pyramid,* the message should be that the transition will be as gradual as possible, minimizing the stress to employees. Clear guarantees should be given about what working conditions will be like after the incremental transition. In the *Cube,* the most important message is that Bridging the "before situation" and the "after situation" ensures that working conditions are as stable as possible. In the *Cylinder,* the message should be that the continual learning process will slowly result in improved working conditions for the people involved. In the *Sphere,* the message is that the portfolio of initiatives, however chaotic, provides the best job guarantees in a turbulent environment.

The second group of Facilitators is the bosses. They are swamped with information, so everything they're told must be crisp and short. One driving force is the extent to which innovation can help them score well on performance indicators. Another is the possibility that they might expand their turf or their career opportunities. A restraining force is that an innovation may not make a specific contribution to their performance indicators; they may feel they have something to lose and nothing to gain. The messages they need to receive are precisely how many people they must provide to help in the innovation and what the impact will be on their performance indicators.

In the *Pyramid,* this means they will have to understand what is gained by going through incremental change. They have to understand that the transition will be as gradual as possible, minimizing disruption in their departments. In the *Cube,* they must be told that good preparation will keep the transition period as short as possible, minimizing potential disruption. In the *Cylinder,* they must understand what activities are planned for the Doers in the cycle and for future cycles. In the *Sphere,* open communication is essential so they can understand and spot the opportunities. Messages must keep stressing values and vision, so they understand how all the initiatives fit into the big picture.

The Doers. The Doers are the most directly involved, so their receptivity and knowledge is the highest of all the segments, and they have the best view of the internal effects of the turbulence. One driving force is that they are in the picture while leading the innovation and will share the fun of being part of it. Another is the personal improvement they will realize by aiding the innovation. A restraining force is the unclear future they may see for their positions and their lack of control over their futures as they go through the transition. These people need to have all the information available on the turbulence and their role in it: they need the detail. They also need some guarantees of their situation after the transition or innovation.

In the *Pyramid,* this means close contact must be maintained because their work will change during the slow and incremental improvements. In the *Cube,* this means providing, during periods of calm, clear guarantees on Bridging over the transition. During the transition, they must be told the different expectations for their activities and for their tasks in the transition. In the *Cylinder,* communication must stress that each cycle's performance needs to exceed all previous cycles', stimulating the incremental improvements. In the *Sphere,* the message is that limited amounts of risks can—and need to—be taken for the good of the company, stimulating experimentation. Make sure they understand that they are the ones who keep the company stable in the turbulent environment, so while managed risks are fine, don't bet the company.

The Supporters. Supporters hear a lot of internal gossip and they get some information from colleagues who are directly involved. Their driving force is a clear improvement in their work position. The major restraining force is the worry that their work might be changed. Special attention must be paid to this group, spelling out the effects that the transition or innovation will have on their situation and, when possible, offering some guarantees. Show them, "Your company really cares for its employees." Show this by handling the turbulence to minimize the impact on them.

In the *Pyramid*, the Supporters' situation can be shown clearly, and they need to understand the limits of the modest support requested from them. In the *Cube*, make sure this group understands that it is not threatened with going through the transition. These people need to be reminded of the role and position they will have after the transition. It must be stressed that the transition period will be kept as short as possible to minimize disruption. In the *Cylinder*, it is important that this group understand that it will receive a pat on the back when a successful cycle is completed and that recognition is not reserved only for those directly involved. In the *Sphere*, ensure that communication taps into the experience of this group, keeping its members involved in going through the different initiatives. These people must understand the importance of providing information to the people doing the different initiatives, which means they must have a certain level of awareness of all the initiatives going on. They need to be persuaded to support their colleagues while going through the transition; roles could be reversed next time and they might be the ones going through the initiatives.

A special group of Supporters is the employees at the client interface, often a forgotten group. The main characteristic of this group is that it is swamped with information because it gets all the information on new products, new services, and more. These people also bear the brunt of customer complaints when, during the transition or innovation, things do not go as smoothly as expected. The main message to these people is that they must understand all the effects on customers and help to pave the way if the initiatives get off to a rocky start. In all four stability structures, this message is similar.

As we mentioned, while tailored communication shapes some messages to specific segments, it shapes other messages for specific times (the timing is closely linked to the shock absorbers of Bridge, Creep, and Surge that were discussed in Chapters 6 and 7) (Figure 42.1).

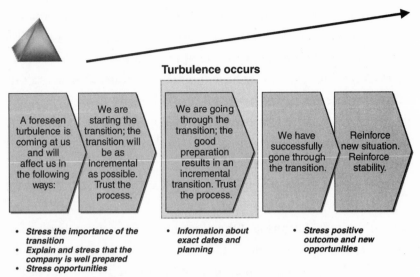

Turbulence occurs

| A foreseen turbulence is coming at us and will affect us in the following ways: | We are starting the transition; the transition will be as incremental as possible. Trust the process. | We are going through the transition; the good preparation results in an incremental transition. Trust the process. | We have successfully gone through the transition. | Reinforce new situation. Reinforce stability. |

- Stress the importance of the transition
- Explain and stress that the company is well prepared
- Stress opportunities

- Information about exact dates and planning

- Stress positive outcome and new opportunities

Figure 42.1 Determine the timing of communication: 1.

In the *Pyramid* it's extremely important to support the Creep—and to help everybody understand that it is necessary to start far in advance of the anticipated event. In fact, that's the biggest challenge for innovating in a Pyramid: to persuade people not to keep waiting but to start doing well in advance. You must stress the importance of incremental improvement and the importance of starting now. Once the initiative is under way, everyone must receive this message: "Trust the process. Because we have gone through this process before, we know it works. Make sure you help it." As you reach milestones, celebrate.

In the *Cube,* the shock absorber used is the Surge (Figure 42.2). During periods of calm, messages should emphasize that people must stay unfrozen. Build camaraderie and prepare them for the next transition by training them. In a communication before the Surge, make sure people understand the Bridging that is in place, because it will help them to take this leap. Once the Surge has begun, focus on what remains the same. Stress the importance of and the appropriateness of the transition, and explain that the transition will be as short as possible with the minimal amount of disruption. It's essential that everybody have the mental model of trusting one another while going through the transition. By explaining these elements, you ensure that disruption will be minimized during the Surge. After successfully going through the cycle, consolidate and prepare for new transitions.

In the *Cylinder,* you support the Surge at the start and at the end of the cycle and the Creep over all the cycles (Figure 42.3). At the start, explain the expectations and the planning to the people involved in this cycle, so they know where and how they fit in. During the cycle, whatever plan was made must not be forgotten. At the end of the cycle, smooth the Surge by celebrating the accomplishment. This enables people to let go of the cycle they were in. Be sure to stress the opportunities of getting on board for the next cycle. Reinforce the

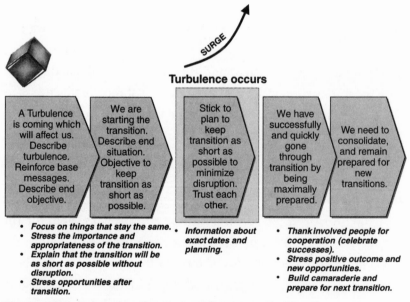

Figure 42.2 Determine the timing of communication: 2.

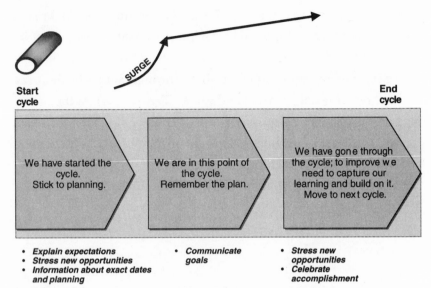

Figure 42.3 Determine the timing of communication: 3.

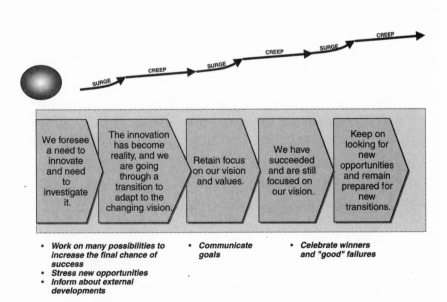

Figure 42.4 Determine the timing of communication: 4.

Creep to foster incremental improvements over the cycle. Make sure the needed learning is captured by having an evaluation session before moving to the next cycle.

In the *Sphere*, support people going through Surges by focusing on what remains stable: vision and values (Figure 42.4). At the beginning of the surge, stress the opportunity that the initiatives provide; at the end, celebrate the winners and the "good failures." Celebrating both makes it much easier for people to let go of what they were doing and move on. Communicating this will help support them through these Surges.

CHAPTER 43

Crisis!

Many managers prepare for a crisis but fail to rehearse for one

The second aspect of communication that varies by stability structure is *Crisis Communication,* which reduces disruptions by informing people quickly and reducing their uncertainty. However good you are at creating stability, crises will occur from time to time, and when they do, good crisis communication is crucial for stability. Prepared and rehearsed Crisis Communication plans can support the stability structures.

Let's consider a few possible crises: A major distributor refuses to handle your product. New products are introduced that redefine a market. Two large competitors unexpectedly agree to merge. New government regulations are announced. An external consultant abandons your IT implementation project, sharply increasing the amount of time it will take to complete it. A factory burns down or a technological breakthrough renders your current project obsolete. New turbulence suddenly emerges, requiring more resources than are available because too many people are involved in other initiatives.

Underestimating the importance of Crisis Communication in any of these situations will result in people receiving incomplete information. That can set off a whole circuit of rumors, which itself creates disruption. The goal is to minimize disruption when a crisis erupts. The key to reaching this goal is to go beyond preparation of a Crisis Communication plan to *rehearsing* it. Rehearsing is necessary to check and improve the plan. Not many companies rehearse their communication plans, and in crisis often make communication blunders that only add to their problems.

Preparing and rehearsing a plan ensures that everybody involved in the Crisis Communication knows their roles and that the company has a coherent story ready for the outside world. Identify possible crisis situations and ask, "What are the consequences? Who would notice?" A chip maker that suffers a production line breakdown might need to reassure customers and investors. A chip maker that suffers an acid spill at a factory, killing six workers and polluting a stream, must deal with a far broader audience of interested parties.

So calculate: What needs to be done? Who needs to be informed? Which groups need to be told when? How do we inform them? What is our message? Are the existing channels of communication useful? Does each involved person know what to do and when to do it? Will the message reach the necessary parties in time? What are the next steps?

We won't go into detail on how to make a Crisis Communication plan, but we do want to note how each structure handles Crisis Communication differently.

In the *Pyramid*, Crisis Communication entails "Stay calm, keep working, we'll handle it." Internal communication will be done by standard e-mail to all people, providing a basic list of questions and answers. This will reassure employees and allow them to pass that information on to family, friends, and neighbors. The main message is "everything is under control." External communication should be handled by one small group that deals with the press and other media.

In the *Cube*, Crisis Communication should be very task oriented, a "do this" approach. Internally the focus is on reminding people of the shared vision and creating passion for it: "We won't be beaten by this drawback. We will keep moving, and we will get there." External communication should be carried out by one specialized department that will determine what information is given out.

In the *Cylinder*, Crisis Communication is first directed at the team involved: "All hands on deck." Internal communication must be intensive and very quick because all the people in the cycle will have a lot of external communicating to do since they talk to many people about the cycle. External communication is done by all the people in the cycle to the different groups outside.

In the *Sphere,* Crisis Communication can be typified as "combine forces" to deal with the crisis. Internal communication will be open; everybody will be informed quickly to ensure that all plans are modified to reflect the crisis at hand. The sole external communication will be, "This is business as usual. In this very turbulent world, many unexpected things happen. This is just one of them."

AIDE MÉMOIRE

1. Teamwork, quality, and communication can help in doing things in the *right ways* to maximize stability. The aspect of *Teamwork* that provides a great leverage point for maximizing stability is to create an environment in which individuals can excel. For *Quality* it's a question of creating safe environments where groups progressively learn to innovate. For *Communication* it's tuning communications to the specific requirements of different stability structures so as to align behavior across the whole organization.

2. Teams based on individuals, or I-teams, can play a substantial role in creating stability through:
   - Focusing on the "I." The tool of choice is the *SWIP Mirror,* which helps individuals plan their futures and helps teams plan for their individuals.
   - *Managing the Marketplace,* creating an environment in which individuals are encouraged to form and work together in I-teams, based on optimizing the *adding value to* and *gaining value from* principle.
   - *Balancing the Biorhythms,* creating a natural balance for individuals, teams, and the organization by insisting on balanced structure and timing of events.

3. *Quality Assurance* acts as a stabilizer that provides guidance on achieving goals and preempts surprises in process and content. QA facilitates cross-fertilization of ideas, and it spots gaps and overlaps in activities. Three Quality tools promote stability amid turbulence:
   - *Canaries* provide an early warning system to reduce troubleshooting and improve performance.
   - *Prototyping the Environment* allows the acceleration of learning in a safe way.
   - *Master-Apprentice Relationships* minimize disruption by creating learning relationships that boost effectiveness and efficiency.

4. Communication helps align behavior during turbulence and increases the responsiveness of your organization and its people by helping them quickly understand what is going on. Two classic forms of business communication differ for each of the stability structures:

- *Tailored Communication* provides people with information relevant to their positions. This targeting can prevent information overload. It also helps align individuals' behavior as they deal with turbulence and go through innovation.

- *Crisis Communication* reduces disruption by informing people quickly about what's going on. This dampens uncertainty and increases people's responsiveness.

Part 4

The Bigger Picture

CHAPTER 44

From structure to structure

Learning to migrate to where you want to be

Up to this point, we've diagnosed organizations, refined the boundaries within them, and decided which are the most effective stability structures to use in the different parts. We've shown how to embed in these domains various shock-absorbing techniques that reinforce stability. We examined how to foster a mental model of stable innovation throughout the organization and how stability can be reinforced by drawing on strategy, tactics, operations, teamwork, quality, and communication. As a final step on this path to stability, we must consider how to move from where you find yourself now to where you would like to be.

As with any planned change, this migration should be done in a way that minimizes disruption. As you contemplate a migration from one stability structure to another, you are dealing with some complex factors. Boundaries may have to be redrawn around some subprocesses to bring together areas sharing the same pattern of innovation. The environments in which people work may change—and if the unwritten rules change too dramatically or too extremely, change fatigue is likely to result. People who fit well in the culture of one form of stable innovation may not fit so well in another. Some may feel forced to leave; others may lose their motivation. This "tissue rejection" might cost you some of your best people.

Consider, for a moment, our four stability structures. Each has an optimal management style associated with it (Figure 44.1):

- Pyramid—the Custodian
- Cube—the Renovator
- Cylinder—the Expert
- Sphere—the Adventurer

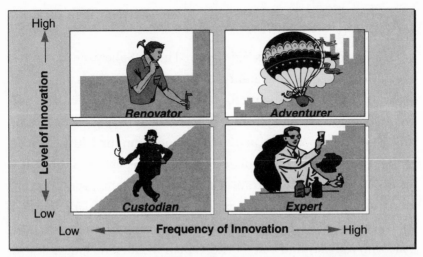

Figure 44.1 There are optimal management styles associated with each of the four forms of stable innovation.

Like the structures themselves, each management style has significant and fundamental differences from the others. The Custodian enjoys sustaining and building strength and solidarity through a steady progression with no surprises. The Renovator enjoys regularly rebuilding the business and focuses first on the effectiveness of the transition and only then on the efficiency of the consolidation. The Expert enjoys pushing back frontiers and views professionalism as a combination of expertise and access to those new challenges. The Adventurer enjoys tackling exciting new opportunities and values flexibility and opportunism.

Many people, we know, display a combination of all four traits. In fact, it would be unusual to find someone who is a pure form of only one style. Yet it's also fair to say that most people feel more comfortable in one or two of the stability structures than in the others. Should they be moved from an environment in which they are comfortable to one that is extremely different, you might wind up with a bad fit that costs you their productivity and their devotion (Figure 44-2).

If a Custodian in a Pyramid is moved into a Sphere, he or she may become confused by an inability to get things done. This person will probably be seen as very political, pedantic, numbers-oriented, and risk-averse. Someone moving from a Sphere to a Pyramid is likely to feel stifled and will probably be perceived as a loose cannon with no respect for status, someone who is politically inept. Each person, ideally suited for the stability structure from which she or he came, winds up in a totally unsupportive environment. So should you consider migration, always bear in mind that if you migrate a domain too far from its original form, you may find that the individuals within it no longer fit with what it has become. And senior leadership may not understand.

As a stability structure migrates, it starts to warp (see Chapters 8 and 9). In other words it takes on some of the characteristics of another struc-

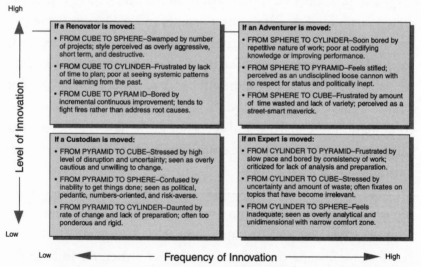

Figure 44.2 People who fit well in the culture of one form of stable innovation may not fit so well in another and may leave if they are forced into it.

FROM SPHERE TO CYLINDER—1

"Fresh Blood"

"You would not *believe* the sort of people I'm managing!" Max waved his coffee mug above the kitchen table in a gesture of disbelief. "I mean, God alone knows how the company ever managed to get to be so successful. They're all so *amateurish*. The founder couldn't create a strategy to get out of a wet paper bag . . ."

His wife looked back sympathetically. "I guess that's why he brought you in and pays you the big bucks, my darling. I mean, for him to bring in a new CEO from the outside rather than hand over to one of the people who helped him start the company must mean he realizes how bad they all are."

Max looked reflective. "It's not so much that they're bad, Lynda. They're not. They're among the most motivated bunch I've ever seen. And incredibly bright. *Very* creative, imaginative . . . great potential. But they're so *undisciplined*. It's not that there's no strategy for the company. There are as many different strategies as there are employees. And they're all clever enough to see the flaws in everyone else's proposals. So they all do their own thing!"

"But isn't that sort of 'self-starting' ability a good thing in today's business? The press is always going on about the need for empowerment and creating conditions for innovation. I thought that was how today's businesses were supposed to stay responsive. Sounds like your people already have it, so that's good isn't it?"

"Maybe when they started. Maybe even a few years ago. But they're in a different league now. They have to compete with players who've been in the business much longer than they have—companies that have *experience* of how the marketplace changes and how to respond. My people always solve each problem from first principles, as if no one has ever had to solve it before. Which isn't true."

Lynda refilled her tea cup. "You know, I wouldn't be at all surprised if they *liked* reinventing the wheel. It can be a lot more fun and exciting than using someone else's work. It's a classic reason for not-invented-here syndrome. It's exactly what you do whenever you try to recreate one of my brilliant recipes."

"*Sometimes* my version tastes better . . ." Max started defensively.

"And sometimes even the cat won't touch it. But that's my point. You don't follow my precise and efficiently documented instructions partly because you know they're 'only' mine, and partly because you're good enough in the kitchen yourself that you could probably have come up with something even better if you only set your mind to it. At work your people are just the same. You're coming in telling them they need to document their procedures . . ."

"They *do* need to, desperately!"

". . . codify lessons learned, share knowledge better, formalize business processes—all the things, frankly, that must sound pretty unexciting and even stifling to them—all in the name of *efficiency*. Well, I bet that many of them joined the company to be at the cutting edge, or change the world, or make a bundle and retire at 40. But I bet *none* of them joined as a result of a deep, burning desire to *be efficient!*"

The couple glared across the table at each other, not quite knowing whether they were having a debate or starting a row. Then Max broke the silence in a serious voice. "The way that the business world is going . . ." then changed his tone as he decided to end the discussion, ". . . they may not have a choice."

Lynda smiled a quick smirk of triumph as she got up. "Don't you believe it," she shot back over her shoulder. "Any people as smart—and as attractive in the job market—as this bunch, *always* have a choice!"

ture. But there are no guarantees either that the warped form will be sustainable or that the direction of the migration is compatible with the characteristics of those working in the original structure. For instance, we saw in Figure 9-2 that a Pyramid could not sustain Spherical characteristics—that is, a Pyramid-Sphere is not a valid warped structure, the least because the Bridging in a Pyramid stifles the free flow needed in a Sphere. Similarly, we know from Figure 44-2 that someone with Custodian traits (suited to a Pyramid) may find a Sphere highly confusing and risky. Combine both factors and you can see that attempting to migrate directly from a Pyramid to a Sphere is fraught with difficulties. So not every theoretical migration is a valid and practical route (Figure 44.3). Some routes are inherently disruptive however you approach them. How much freedom do you have to move?

It depends. Our experience is that if you want to move horizontally along the matrix—changing the frequency of innovation—that is quite possible to do in a nondisruptive transition, either by a sustained Surge or by a combination of Surge and Creep. If you want to move vertically

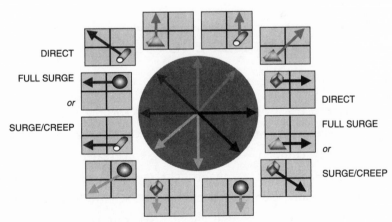

DIRECT

FULL SURGE

or

SURGE/CREEP

DIRECT

FULL SURGE

or

SURGE/CREEP

DIRECT PARTIAL SURGE FOLLOWED BY DISRUPTIVE SNAP
or INDIRECT FULL SURGE

Figure 44.3 The possibility for a direct nondisruptive transition between stability structures depends on the move.

up the matrix—increasing the level of innovation—that is *impossible* to do directly without disruption. The only way to increase the level of innovation without subjecting your employees to disruption is to choose an indirect root; that is, to migrate first to a different stability structure and then on to your ultimate goal. Of course this makes the whole transition longer and more complex, and so increases the risk of unintentionally nevertheless crossing the disruption threshold (see Figure 5-1).

Moving down the matrix—decreasing the level of innovation—is possible by a direct route, but only partially. It involves a Surge and a disruptive snap as the warped stability structure is wrenched into a new form in the last stage of its transition. If that sounds unpleasant, imagine how it feels to employees as the organization intentionally (albeit temporarily) crosses the disruption threshold, invoking immediate change fatigue.

Other migratory routes involve diagonal movement within the matrix, changing both the level of innovation and the frequency of innovation. The level of disruption will reflect which transition you are attempting. If you are decreasing the frequency but increasing the level

---

FROM SPHERE TO CYLINDER—2

"Roll Over and Die"

Max was clearly shocked as he leaned across the desk toward his 52-year-old chairman. "John, I can't believe you're saying you want to leave the company—*your* company. You created this place. It's your baby. Even after you brought me in to run it, it always remained yours. Even after all the changes I've introduced, everyone always sees you as the figurehead. *I* see you as the figurehead, dammit! Why leave? I thought we were getting on so well! Is it something I've done? What . . . ? I . . ." He ran out of steam.

"Hey, hey, don't take it so to heart, my friend." John leaned forward, patted Max on the arm, and then sat back again. "It's nothing about you. Nothing *wrong* anyway. It's the place, the company, the feel. It's not what I created."

"But I was brought in to *change* what you created! You told me . . ."

"I know, I *know!* You've done a great job. Just what I wanted," he hesitated, half smiled, "well, if I'm honest, just what the company *needed* would be more accurate. I knew that all the fun of the start-up was over for good once we had a head count of more than 50. By the time we topped 100, we were creaking at the seams. That's when I knew we needed fresh blood at the top. Someone who could bring some order to chaos. Someone who could herd the cats! Bring some discipline to how we conducted business. That person was—and is—you. A good choice then, and a good choice now."

"Well then, why go? Why leave when things are really picking up, when we've got record performance? We're just getting what you wanted and you're walking out on us? Just like Joe the other month. And Christine before. You guys built this place. I just don't get it."

"No! We did *not* build this place. We built what came before this place. And we enjoyed that place—even while knowing in our hearts that the wildness, the feeling of freedom, the adolescent almost cowboy lifestyle, couldn't last."

"But that was a question of size, and the market . . ."

"Of course! All the business reasons behind the strategy you introduced 2 years ago—and which I still support—were correct. Are correct. And for a long while I assumed that I wanted to be a part of the new 'grown-up' company. And until about 6 months ago that remained true. We steadily became more disciplined, more focused, more procedural, and that was OK. But then at the start of this year suddenly everything seemed to speed up. It was like when overnight your voice drops, and you start shaving regularly, and you can't be a kid any more, and you feel silly and childish and embarrassed if you try. So you snap over to being a grown up. And as a company we seemed to do the same thing.

"I think it was about the time we introduced the annual review process. Suddenly everything seemed to click. All at once the annual cycle seemed to be driving everything. Before, we'd never had an annual *anything* other than the summer party. Within 2 months the new *Employee Manual* was published with a best practice for *everything* it seemed. New junior recruits were only brought in once a year so they could all be "inducted" as a group. And I went along to the first group, thinking I'd talk about the 'feel' of the company—the company that I knew.

"And I suddenly realized that all those new recruits would *love* the grown-up company but would never know what the adolescent company had felt like. And they didn't need to. *They* were the grown-up company." His eyes glistened, although his expression didn't change. ". . . and I was not. And what's worse," he added softly, "I didn't really want to be . . ."

of innovation—migrating from Cylinder to Cube—it is possible to do that directly. So is a migration from Cube to Cylinder. Decreasing both the frequency and level of innovation simultaneously (Sphere to Pyramid) is possible if you are willing to accept a certain level of disruption or to take an indirect route. Migrating from Pyramid to Sphere, however, is impossible without significant disruption. Increasing both the frequency of innovation and its level is too extreme a transition to manage nondisruptively.

Based on our experiences to date, we have compiled a set of "roadmaps" to act as guidelines when planning migration paths. The sequence of the roadmaps presented here is from relatively simple transitions to progressively more difficult ones. Clearly, however, although in coming up with the sequence we were able to corroborate our experience against a theoretical underpinning (based on stability of warped forms and compatibility of character traits), the specific order is necessarily wholly subjective.

The easiest migrations are the six direct routes that can be achieved all by Surge *or* by a combination of Surge/Creep.

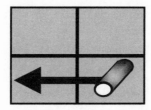

The easiest changes to stability structures are changes in frequency of innovation (horizontal migrations on the matrix). A shift from Cylinder to Pyramid can be started by using the end-of-cycle Surge of the Cylinder. At the end of each cycle, the changes needed to warp the Cylinder to have more Pyramidal characteristics (such as greater Bridging, more incremental processes) are Surged into place. However, as more and more Bridging is installed, so it becomes increasingly difficult to Surge without cracking into a Lewin change. Nevertheless, by this time incremental change has largely taken over from cyclical change, so Creep becomes the means to complete the transition. Toward the completion of the transition, even Creeping will become progressively more difficult to maintain without disruption as Pyramidal stability gains in dominance and heavy Bridging builds.

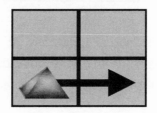

Migrating from Pyramid to Cylinder involves an initial slow Creep to reduce Bridging. This, however, requires significant attention to avoid too much disruption in Enablers and Triggers (typically resulting in symptoms of confusion and insecurity) as the heavy Bridging of the Pyramid is partially dismantled. However, conventional Creep becomes very much easier once the migration has started. Once Cylindrical stability dominates, it is possible to progressively Surge the end of the transition. This Surge is not continuous but is instead pulsed in time with the intended cycle of the eventual Cylinder.

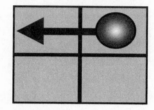

Similar migration patterns occur for the other two lateral moves. To shift from Sphere to Cube, a Surge can be maintained throughout. However, it gets progressively more difficult to avoid disruption as Cubic stability gains in dominance and Bridging builds. Therefore, the Surge needs to be taken progressively slowly. This can cause problems if top management perceives the slowing as a gradual "losing of steam" and reacts by trying to reaccelerate the migration.

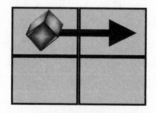

Full migration of a Cube to Sphere can be achieved with a single Surge. In an exact mirror to the migration in the opposite direction, the start of the transition demands great management attention to avoid perceived disruption. The problem here is that top management, fired up with enthusiasm, pushes the change too hard too soon. An additional problem can be that employees' expectations are not managed correctly so that people become cynical about the practicality of the changes because they are initially so slow. The temptation at this point to risk the change fatigue of a Lewin change can be quite high. However, if the early stages of this migration are handled correctly, the remainder becomes very much easier as Bridging is removed and Spherical stability dominates.

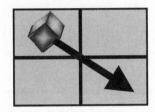

We now come to the migrations to and from Cubic and Cylindrical forms. Changing from Cube to Cylinder is potentially one of the easiest migrations because it is executed in a single Cubic Surge. The shift to Cylindrical form simply becomes the goal of the Cube on its next Surge. The problems of this migration have more to do with the complexity of designing the desired Cylinder (involving as it does an increase in frequency of innovation) and the different character traits required by people in a Cylinder (such as skill in pattern recognition to learn from the past).

The last of the relatively easy migrations is from Cylinder to Cube. Here migration is probably best executed by means of progressively lengthening the end-of-cycle Surges of the Cylinder—slowing the "clock rate" if you will. However, you will find that it takes significant effort to maintain the intermediate warped forms.

More difficult migrations require either indirect routes or else Surging followed by a disruptive "snap."

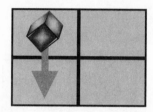

Although reducing the level of innovation from a Cube to a Cylinder was one of the easiest migrations, ironically the other three vertical movements down the matrix are much more difficult and must either be achieved by taking indirect routes or else by voluntarily accepting temporary disruption. Migrating from Cube to Pyramid involves initially Surging (using the Surge capability for which the Cube is designed) but then *either* splitting structures when Pyramidal stability starts to dominate (if Cubic stability is to be maintained) *or* letting the structure disruptively snap to Pyramidal stability with heavy Bridging. Alternatively you can take an indirect nondisruptive route via a Cylinder structure. In other words, in a single Surge migrate the Cube into a Cylinder with a very slow innovation rate, and then rapidly enhance incremental improvement processes and general Bridging. As with all indirect routes, it is always dubious as to whether the extra time and confusion caused is worth it. Probably only extreme existing change fatigue combined with the luxury of a medium-term time horizon can justify using intermediate routes—unless there are some useful side effects that can be accrued by migrating via the intermediate form. A company might choose to take a department along the Cube to

Cylinder to Pyramid route, for instance, if it felt that the "slow spinning Cylinder" phase would help build the organizational learning needed by the Pyramid.

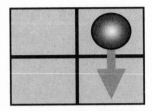

A similar decision process is needed for the two remaining reductions in level of innovation. Moving a Sphere to Cylinder involves initial Surging followed by the choice *either* to split structures when Cylindrical stability starts to dominate (if Spherical stability is to be maintained) *or* to let the warped structure disruptively snap to Cylindrical stability with significant Bridging. Alternatively, you can take an indirect nondisruptive route via Cube structure—with all the same caveats as before.

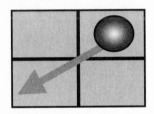

Migrating from Sphere to Pyramid necessarily involves temporary disruption because the only indirect nondisruptive route would be via Cube *and* Cylinder, which to all intents and purposes is impractical. The only reasonable route is to start Surging and then *either* split structures when Pyramidal stability starts to dominate (if Spherical stability is to be maintained) *or* let the structure disruptively snap to Pyramidal stability with heavy Bridging.

The most difficult migrations can only be achieved by taking indirect routes or jumping.

Although Cylinders can make progressive pulses to simultaneously reduce frequency of innovation at the same time as increasing
level of innovation (and so migrate to Cubes), all other migrations
involving *increased* levels of innovation are extremely problematic.

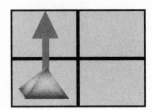

The easiest way of shifting from Pyramid to Cube is probably to
immediately set up a separate Cube, shut down the original Pyramid,
and be done with it. An alternative is to set up a separate warped
Cube-Pyramid and then Surge to the pure Cube. Alternatively, take an
indirect (theoretically) nondisruptive route via a Cylinder structure—
with all the usual soul searching beforehand.

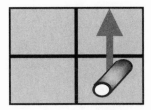

Shifting from a Cylinder to Sphere entails a similar decision tree:
Immediately set up separate Sphere *or* set up a separate Sphere-Cylinder
and then Surge to the Sphere. Alternatively, consider taking a potentially
nondisruptive, though protracted, route via a Cube structure.

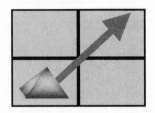

With the final—and most difficult—transition, Pyramid to Sphere, your hands are tied. The only theoretical indirect nondisruptive route is via Cylinder *and* Cube, so (as with the Sphere-to-Pyramid migration) is impractical. The only options left are to immediately set up a separate Sphere *or* set up a separate Sphere-Pyramid and then Surge to a Sphere.

On balance, then, you can see that many migration routes are possible without any perceived disruption to those involved. The risk of a cultural misfit nevertheless makes some more attractive than others. Of the remaining routes, it's a choice between accepting a limited amount of disruption or taking longer and putting in more management effort to go through an intermediate stage. The ultimate decision should be made not by slavishly following the preceding roadmaps, but by using them to think through the options, risks, and trade-offs associated with each migration in the context of why the migration was attractive in the first place.

CHAPTER 45

Seagulls in a growing storm

Competence in building stability will become the basis for competition

Throughout this book, we have urged you to concentrate on maximizing stability with innovation built in, rather than fixating on change. As we said in the opening paragraphs, in the current global economy an organization has to maximize stability structure to thrive amid turbulence. The Pyramid, Cube, Cylinder, and Sphere need to be built into a portfolio that can be used by the different domains in your organization for all the turbulence they are sure to encounter. We've discussed how to build the right forms of stable innovation into your organization by analyzing the potential disruptions that each domain will face and using the appropriate combinations of Bridging, Creeping, and Surging to create the appropriate stability structures.

As you look out the window, watch the television, go online, read your favorite publications, hear the announcements of your business rivals . . . you are all too aware that the world is not static. The value of your company increasingly depends on your ability to minimize the disruption caused by growing turbulence. The Lewin change model (unfreeze/move/freeze) has, we believe, the wrong focus. People's resentment and fatigue from the frequent wrenching changes will undermine your organization. Instead of the Lewin way, do it *the stable way*.

Increasing productivity increases your company's value. Productivity rests on your ability to minimize disruption. For many companies, handling turbulence by change initiatives is a significant business activity with a particularly low return. *Stability* offers a better way:

1. Structure innovation in line with your business environment to minimize disruption. This makes thriving in turbulence easier because you build the most necessary innovations into your organization.

2. Use the shock-absorption techniques to maintain aligned Enabler/Trigger mechanisms. This eliminates disruption, and therefore the direct cause of change fatigue. It also sharply reduces resistance to change.

3. Set up stabilizers in strategy, tactics, operations, teamwork, quality, and communication to perform structured handling of innovation. This increases the ease of handling turbulence because it introduces the mental model of stability into your everyday business.

The result? A better alignment of actions and knowledge. This reduces the level of frustration caused by change resistance and leads to better performance. Productivity increases because there are fewer setbacks and an increased chance of success for each initiative for handling turbulence. Productivity increases because people understand the direction of innovations, and their actions are better aligned. People are better able to set priorities and plan their activities. Stress about change and distraction is reduced, leading to better performance.

Most companies do not come close to making the necessary changes. Unable to deal with increasing turbulence, companies lose their competitive edge. Soon their boards of directors and the financial markets are demanding reassurance about their competency to maintain stability.

So in the long term, the value of your company will directly reflect how well it thrives in turbulence. Your employees' performance is likely to be affected by their perception of disruption. This perception of "employee care" travels quickly through the company, as well as outside it, as employees' perceptions are reported in news coverage and discussed at parties. If perceptions sour, your best people will be among the first to leave because they are the most mobile. The best people outside the company will have little interest in joining it.

As the world becomes increasingly turbulent, as the global economy heats up, as life becomes more hectic, competence in building stability will become the basis for competition. Building in innovation without disruption will be the way to create sustainable competitive advantages. Those companies with the competence to manage a portfolio of stability structures will lead the game.

At the front of the pack will be companies that choose to compete only in those areas that fit like a glove—where the product-market combinations are not only attractive but fit with the stability structures of your company. Only now can we so clearly understand the factors that affect that fit—the factors critical to avoiding change fatigue and corporate burn-out. Only now is it possible to position yourself on the value chain and base your outsourcing strategy on your competence in dealing with turbulence—keeping in house those activities that match the dominant innovation patterns for which the related domains are tuned and outsourcing the rest.

Like seagulls in a growing storm, companies must become masterful at maximizing stability amid turbulence. Some gulls will struggle to survive. The most skillful will ride the winds, drawing on their experience and applying the techniques perfected in milder weather. These best will know how to anticipate major currents, how to spot and avoid obstacles, and how to respond rapidly and vigorously to unexpected updrafts and downdrafts. The less experienced and less skillful will waste too much energy fighting the storm and will eventually exhaust themselves.

We need to learn from the seagulls. A storm is looming.

Index

About the Authors

Peter Scott-Morgan is the best-selling author of *The Unwritten Rules of the Game* and is well known as a popular business speaker, consultant and teacher. He is globally recognized as an authority on managing revolutionary transformation in business. With a New Economy lifestyle he lives in the Caribbean in winter and the English Riviera in summer. In his spare time Dr. Scott-Morgan is a partner of the international consultancy Arthur D. Little, Inc., and Professor of Business at Boston's ADL School of Management. Find out more @ www.scott-morgan.com.

Erik Hoving is a partner in the Rotterdam office of Arthur D. Little, Inc. He leads the Telecommunications, Information Technology, Media, and Electronics practice. In this extremely exciting world he is especially interested in issues concerning strategy and organization, entrepreneurship, and innovation. Before he joined Arthur D. Little, he worked for AT&T Network Systems International, which is now known as Lucent Technologies.

Henk Smit is a partner in the Rotterdam office of Arthur D. Little, Inc., specializing in implementing product and business innovation, managing business transformation, and embedding corporate change. Throughout the 1990s he worked closely with international firms, frequently on a long-term basis, to realize profound change. His experience covers a wide range of industries in services and manufacturing, including telecommunications, consumer products, and automotive.

Arnoud van der Slot is a partner in the Rotterdam office of Arthur D. Little, Inc. Within Arthur D. Little he is responsible worldwide for the methodologies to deal with complex change programs. During the last 10 years he was involved in transforming utility, telecom, and energy corporations.